HUNGER

Other books by Jon Dybdahl:
Adventist Mission in the Twenty-first Century
A Strange Place for Grace

To order, call **1-800-765-6955**.

Visit us at
www.AutumnHousePublishing.com
for information on other Autumn House® products.

JON L. DYBDAHL

Published by Autumn House® Publishing, a division of Review and Herald® Publishing, Hagerstown, MD 21741-1119

Autumn House® titles may be purchased in bulk for educational, business, fund-raising, or sales promotional use. For information, e-mail SpecialMarkets@reviewandherald.com.

Autumn House® Publishing publishes biblically based materials for spiritual, physical, and mental growth and Christian discipleship.

The author assumes full responsibility for the accuracy of all facts and quotations as cited in this book.

This book was
Edited by Gerald Wheeler
Copyedited by James Cavil
Cover design by Trent Truman
Cover art composite: Man kneeling/SermonView.com;
iStockphoto.com/swaite/ggodby/ANGELGILD/graphixil
Interior design by Heather Rogers
Typeset: Bembo 11/14

PRINTED IN U.S.A.

12 11 10 09 08 5 4 3 2 1

Library of Congress Cataloging-in-Publication Data
Dybdahl, Jon.
Hunger: satisfying the longing of your soul/Jon Dybdahl.
p. cm.
1. Spirituality—Adventists. 2. Dybdahl, Jon. 3. Spiritual biography. I. Title.
BV4501.3.D93 2007
248.4'86732—dc22
2007025015

ISBN 978-0-8127-0458-7

Dedication

To Kathy:

Beloved wife
Wise confidant
Compassionate nurse
Spiritual teacher

43 years seems like a day

Contents

Introduction

This book proposes a new (yet old) definition of religion that may take you by surprise. When you realize its implications, you may find yourself shocked. On the other hand, you may feel a sense of coming home.

For at least the past century, with roots going back much earlier, most of the Christian West has defined itself by doctrine or dogma. Creeds, confessions, and doctrinal statements described the nature of "faith" (which was basically intellectual assent). While I'm not saying that the interest in doctrines is misplaced, it has often crowded out other aspects of faith.

Christianity should be a way of life—one characterized by communion with God. Jesus was a religious bombshell in people's thoughts because they eventually realized that He was God interacting with humanity. Matthew called Him "Immanuel"—which means "God with us" (Matt. 1:23). The divine/human communion (a close two-way relationship) that humanity had lost in Eden Jesus was now in the process of restoring. When He left our world to return to heaven, He bequeathed His Spirit to His followers. The Holy Spirit was His ongoing presence. God meant Christianity to be an ongoing communion or interaction with Him via Jesus through the Holy Spirit.

This book aims to explain some of this, but even more than that, it seeks to be an invitation to you. I call you to accept this original definition of the Christian religion and decide to live a life of communion with God. I outline suggested steps to satisfy the hunger that the unbalanced interest in and use of doctrines has left in so many lives.

Please go on this journey with me. Some parts of what I say need careful attention and thought. You may not always agree with what I say, but I believe that if you listen and follow it you will find yourself changed.

Special note: *At the beginning of each chapter you will find quotations attributed to "fellow spiritual pilgrims." Who are they? For years as I have taught spiritual formation to students, I have found it to be a two-way street. They teach me too. Their words and papers (these quotes are from them) have also blessed me. Please join us as fellow pilgrims on this spiritual journey.*

Chapter 1

The Universal Hunger

"I sense that my deepest need is to make myself available to God so that He can speak to me. I really want to experience God in a full measure—not in some extraordinary way, but just to be able to feel His presence and guidance."

"Theology may give you information that is important, but it cannot fill the deepest longings of the broken soul."

"There is no journey to God—only a journey with God."

—Fellow Spiritual Pilgrims

An Urgent Hunger

Human hunger for God is intense and universal. Even if suppressed or denied, it cries out silently from the depths. Such hunger is not a wish to know about God, but rather a quest to encounter Him. People want to touch, experience, and feel the divine—not just discover facts about God. While the hunger affects all people, it is especially evident in the Western world, especially those places in which secularism and traditional Christianity have become most prevalent.

I understand the hunger because it has also gripped me. In 1984 I had recently finished doctoral studies in religion and was teaching at a Christian college. Earlier I had suffered a spiritual crisis while serving as a missionary in Thailand. Though raised as a Christian and knowing my beliefs intellectually, I had never come to an experience that told my heart that God had truly accepted me. Serving in another culture upset my equilibrium and brought me to a crisis. In the end, after an intense search and struggle, I found an assurance of forgiveness and acceptance by a gracious God. I had, in common parlance, been "born again." It led, however, to challenging questions. How could one so socially and educationally steeped in Christianity and who had even been "born again" still feel so spiritually hungry and thirsty? I knew that God loved me, but why did I feel distant from Him? What was going on?

I began a search—a not-so-secret quest to find God. The Lord started me down the road by beginning to teach me about worship. He used the simple testimony of one who had seen renewal come to his church through heartfelt worship to awaken me to the wonderful sense of presence that comes as Jesus is adored. God used Quaker Thomas Kelly's story in *A Testament of Devotion*[1] to warm my heart and instruct me. Henri Nouwen intensified the craving.[2] Through them and many other sources I slowly began to recover a sense of God's presence and to transform a devotional life that had once been dry and almost nonexistent, even though I had served as a missionary and pastor.

As I began, at first hesitantly, to speak of what I thought was my solitary search, I quickly learned that I was not alone. Teacher colleagues of mine in other disciplines as well as my own began to talk about their own spiritual hunger. In fear and trembling a colleague and I taught an experimental class on the spiritual life. We took students on a retreat during which in small groups they talked about their spiritual journeys. To our surprise, students flocked to the class. Students of all types in large numbers took the class for general elective credit, something virtually unheard-of. Clearly faculty and students alike shared the same hunger that I had experienced. I clearly remember the response of one student when I asked, "Why are you taking this class?" With clear conviction he said, "All the beliefs we've heard before, but this is what we need for our life."

In the years following I have learned that this hunger is universal in my church. When they receive clear teaching on actually experiencing God, people respond, because it is food for their hungry souls.

The explosion of interest in spirituality in Christianity indicates that my hunger is a universal one in the Christian church. Books on prayer, meditation, Bible study, worship, and other topics of devotional theology have proliferated. Courses in Bible schools and Christian colleges as well as seminars for the general public have rapidly spread. The demand continues to grow.

It is easy to see the same trend in the West even outside the Christian stream. One can easily document the growing popularity of Eastern religions. New Age gurus find an eager hearing, and books and magazines on spiritual topics are popular. The issue today is deciding which spirituality to follow. Television, movies, and other popular media are full of angels, demons, spells, and every imaginable kind of supernatural occurrence. Even if people are not so interested in following traditional religions, at least they'd like to touch divine or supernatural power. The basic hunger is the same.

Reasons for the Hunger

The natural question that one asks at this juncture is "Why is such hunger so acute at this time in the Western world? What drives this insatiable craving?"

Part of the answer is our recent history and culture. As physical hunger results from the absence of food, hunger for God arises out of the absence of the divine. The "enlightenment" period of the past 150 years has intellectually squeezed God out of life. Even where a theoretical belief in God's existence has lingered, He usually has little direct contact with daily life. Science can explain just about everything even for many Christians. A subsequent chapter (12) will explore this in more detail.

Four main factors especially trigger this hunger among Christians and those in societies heavily influenced by the Christian faith. The first results from the way we have defined religion as accepting certain ideas with the mind. We traditionally use statements of belief to explain our brand of religion. Many churches employ such documents as the Apostles' Creed. Denominations in the reformed tradition have "confessions," such as the Westminster Confession. As theology students soon learn, these confessions are not acknowledgments of sin, but statements of doctrinal orthodoxy. Christians use such statements to show their orthodoxy and make clear their differences with other groups. All of these attempts, though, reflect an implied definition of religion that is primarily cognitive and intellectual.

The contrast of this definition of religion with those employed by non-Christians hit me with force one day as I was teaching world religions. Muslims define themselves by five pillars. The first pillar confesses that God is one and that Muhammad is His prophet. Outside of this first pillar, the other four pillars all deal with the spiritual life and not doctrine. They urge prayer five times a day, almsgiving to the poor, Ramadan as the yearly fast, and pilgrimage to Mecca. For a Muslim, then, religion includes some doctrine, but has more to do with the spiritual life than intellectual belief.

Many Hindus and Buddhists describe the particular sect or brand of their faith by the meditation type they follow. All these non-Christian religions, by their very practice, view religion much more as a devotional or spiritual experience than as a philosophy or idea.

Thus it is not strange that many Christians feel a hunger for God because their very definition (often only subconscious) of what religion is cuts them off from the source of spiritual life—communion with God.

The problem becomes even clearer as we look at the second reason for the hunger. The very definition of theology accepted by Christians militates against taking the devotional life seriously. Traditionally many in the church spoke in the plural about theology. There was not *a* theology but *three* major branches of theology. The first, dogmatic or doctrinal theology, dealt with doctrines and philosophy and taught people what to believe. The second, moral theology, concerned ethics and instructed people how to behave toward one another and in society. The third, mystical or devotional theology, focused on the spiritual life and guided people in their religious experience. For most Christians the threefold concept has vanished. Theology has become singular and refers only to the first category. Thus theology in the popular mind has become doctrinal theology almost exclusively. Is it any wonder that for many "theology" seems boring and irrelevant? It should be no surprise, then, that those who delve deeply into the discipline often feel the greatest hunger for God.

The third reason for the spiritual hunger follows naturally. Because of the preceding deeply ingrained understandings of religion and theology, those responsible for teaching Christianity at the highest levels have often neglected to present the spiritual life. Based on a survey in 1994 by the Murdoch Trust of more than 800 people, the importance placed on spirituality and the spiritual life in the life of a pastor varies greatly between laypeople, pastors, and seminary professors.[3] Laypeople list spirituality as the number one priority in a perfect pastor. Pastors rate it number four. Seminary professors do not even rate spirituality as in the top five priorities for pastoral training. Their most important item is theological knowledge. What the average layperson craves does not figure as crucial in the minds of those teaching Christianity at the highest level.

I am a product of this system. From first grade I went to church school and studied required religion and Bible classes. For 16 years I remained in this system until I finished college. Then I began theological studies and attended two different conservative Christian seminaries, finally graduating with a Ph.D. I do not regret that education. It shaped me in many good ways and preserved me from the drug culture and other dangers in society. Also it led me to love the Bible and enjoy theological teaching and discussion. On the other hand, this system was based on the same unbalanced definition of religion I have shared above. During those 20-plus years of Christian education I studied numerous Bible and religion classes and learned the doctrines and the history of Christianity. In the seminary I studied the biblical languages. In all that time I never had one class devoted specifically to instruction and training in the spiritual life. People assumed that I should pray, but they never required me to read a book on prayer or meditation. My teachers were good people, and I believe they thought that I would "catch" the devotional life on my own. While this is now changing, we must admit that several generations were raised in that way, and that legacy unfortunately continues.

Unbalanced Following

The fourth and final reason for the hunger relates to the selective way we have understood and followed our important religious founders. Charismatically gifted founders of religious reforms or movements typically are wholistic in their approach. Martin Luther is a good example of this. In his role as initiator of the German Protestant Reformation he performed many functions, serving as preacher, teacher, writer, and even having a hand in the music created by the new movement. Certainly he wrote and taught theology, and his theology brought renewal. But Luther was much more than a theologian. He was a great promoter of a renewed religious life. As a former monk, he was diligent in prayer and wrote a book on the subject. Regularly spending two or three hours a day in prayer, he had a motto that said, "He that has prayed well has studied well."[4]

With the passing of Luther this balanced approach that combined a renewed doctrinal understanding with an experiential heart communion with God gradually vanished. Lutheranism developed two main branches. The first, confessional or scholastic Lutheranism, preserved the theological heritage of Luther and developed it with ever greater detail.[5] The second branch, Pietism, emphasized the cruciality of a living heart experience of the resurrected Christ. Pietists were fervent in devotion and zealous in evangelism. While Pietism had an influence, confessionalism ultimately triumphed and became mainstream Lutheranism. The original wholistic view of religion faded away.

A similar experience emerged in the experience of John Wesley and Methodism. John Wesley was the complete Reformer. Theologically he subscribed to Reformation theology and the evangelical experience. Clearly teaching the importance of both personal and social holiness, he founded a movement with all the things needed to nurture the spiritual life. His small class meeting system (a maximum of 12 members) and band organization provided a powerful model for personal discipleship and devotion in small groups that required accountability of its members. Wesley's devotion to Jesus led him to spend two hours a day in prayer that usually began at 4:00 a.m.[6]

The death of Wesley also brought changes to Methodism. By the late nineteenth century it had abandoned the "class meeting" and "band" small group systems. Such small dedicated groups that gave structure and accountability to the devotional and spiritual life and had been the basic structure of Methodism now collapsed. Soon, by the middle to late twentieth century, Methodism was probably best known for its dedication to social action. Attempts at reviving the old system have so far been only partially successful.

I have seen a similar thing happen in the Seventh-day Adventist Church with Ellen G. White, founder and prophet. A complete religious reformer, she took a prominent role in the doctrinal reform relating to the literal return of Jesus, the immutability of God' s law, and the wholistic view of humanity. Extensively preaching, teaching, and writing, she led in the founding of schools and the establishment of medical institutions. She had powerful experiences of communion with God, was deeply devotional, and spoke and wrote extensively on the spiritual life in all its aspects.

An examination of the scholarly work on her writings will reveal that after her death Adventists have studied her mostly for what she has to say about doctrinal belief and Christian lifestyle. She has become for most Seventh-day Adventists an arbiter of theological questions and a champion of conservative lifestyle. What I am saying is not to belittle such contributions, but to point out how one-sided they are. You will find almost nothing written about her spirituality and teachings on the devotional life. A couple years ago I had a graduate assistant collect her writing on the subject of repentance and confession. The amount she wrote in this area is staggering, yet the denomination has done little or nothing with this material, because its scholarly interests lie in other subject areas. We could say much the same for other devotional topics.

In an attempt to lessen her impact on theological issues, some have even said that she is "just a devotional writer." They see it as a way to relegate what she says to the prayer room rather than the classroom. That statement "just a devotional writer" has deeply disturbing implications. Is devotional theology any less crucial than dogmatic theology to the life of the church? Is not devotional theology the ultimate outworking of the Christian life? Perhaps we should rather say "just a doctrinal theologian" instead.

All of these factors help us understand why there has developed such a hunger to meet God. The form of Christianity that has controlled the mainstream of the church in the West has leaned too far toward the side of the cognitive intellectual explanation of Christianity. It should come, then, as no surprise that many Christians, even lifelong believers, crave anything that will help them experience God. This also explains why the charismatic/pentecostal forms of Christianity are by far the fastest-growing parts of the Christian church. The very essence of this moment is that God's Spirit is active in the world and the life of the believer, and thus people with an experiential hunger often find fulfillment there.

It also explains why more and more people in the West have sought a religious experience in belief systems other than Christianity. The Christianity that they have seen or heard about is often the mainstream intellectual sort that strikes them as dry, boring, and irrelevant. The latest guru or New Age teaching is very often primarily propagating an experience of religion rather than a doctrine about God. Increasingly postmodern people and others hunger for the direct touch of the divine.

Is Seeking God Valid?

Is it proper for a person to desire deeply and to strive deliberately for an actual encounter with God? Or is this the aim of a lesser soul craving the latest excitement? Could it be a wish for an experience that avoids serious thinking? I have already suggested that spiritual hunger is universal. Is it right to try to satisfy it?

The reason I raise this issue is that many people have asked me this question in different forms. "Shouldn't we just 'believe,'" they ask, "and not try to experience God?" Some have gone even further and argued that the desire for an experience with God is the wish of an immature believer who can't just accept things without seeing them. I suggest that to seek to experience communion with God is not wrong or immature, but is actually following a God-planned path.

For most Christians, perhaps the best way to deal with such questions is to refer them to the Bible. Do believers in the Bible meet God? Do they desire to encounter Him? Do they walk and talk with Him and interact with Him? The answer, of course, is a resounding "Yes!" Indeed, if you carefully read Scripture one of the amazing things that emerges, one that often shocks our culture, is the free and frequent direct communication between God and humanity.

When our family went as missionaries to the mountains of northern Thailand, one of the first major cultural/religious differences we noticed was this very fact—the people expected divine action. They saw God or the evil one at work in daily life. I found that I, the supposed religious teacher, was much more dubious about the Lord's presence and action than those who supposedly needed teaching. Finally I concluded, to my chagrin, that the people I was living among were much more like the biblical saints than I was. While I do not agree with everything they thought, it was good for me to see that they, along with the Bible, truly believed that God acted and could be experienced.

Although we could say much, much more on the topic, but I believe this is sufficient to make the basic point clear. The Bible story, both Old and New Testaments, expects that true religion implies an experience of God's presence. Israelite and Christian faith was and is not just a philosophy based on ideas, but a religion based on an ongoing interaction with God. If He was not relating in a real way with His people, something was wrong.

The Double Longing

The hunger for God is not to be denied, squelched, suppressed, or reasoned away. God has placed it in us to be nurtured, cherished, and satisfied as only He can do. He meant it to draw us on a quest, a search, a pilgrimage to find Him and to be surprised by the discovery that before we began to look for Him, He had already for a long time been seeking us.

As Thad Rutter put it so beautifully, we discover the *double longing.*[7] We learn first that we have a longing—a deep hunger for God and a sense of His presence. As we begin to pursue that intense desire, we encounter a second even stronger longing. God's heart desperately longs for us. That increases even more our desire for Him, and the spiral of communion continues to grow.

Greater understanding of this double longing came to me through our grandson Noah. For a number of months our son and his family, including 3-year-old Noah, lived in our basement. Noah and I were friends, and every morning when he awakened he would come up the stairs calling for me. "Grandpa, Grandpa, where are you? I haven't seen you yet today." Usually I was in my study, and we would talk and play awhile before I had to go to work. As you can imagine I longed to hear that voice every day. I must admit that I even called my office assistant several times to say that I'd be late for work because of a situation at home. Noah had overslept, and I couldn't face the day without that time together. I wanted to meet my grandson even more than he did me. I can only faintly imagine how much God, our heavenly Father, longs to hear our voice reaching out to Him, saying, "Father, Father, where are you? I haven't seen you yet today." That shows the divinely ordained "double longing."

Conclusion

The only way to satisfy the deep spiritual hunger of our age is to pursue the "double longing." That is what this book is about. It invites you in a practical way to cultivate the spiritual path of communion with God that can both meet your longing for Him and allow you to bask in His longing for fellowship with you. If that is happening, all other true religion follows. But if that is missing, all other religious practices are meaningless. Please join me for the journey.

---

[1] Thomas R. Kelly, *A Testament of Devotion* (New York: Harper and Row, 1941).

[2] Henri J. M. Nouwen, *Making All Things New* (San Franscisco: Harper and Row, 1981).

[3] Reproduced in *Christianity Today*, Oct. 24, 1994, p. 75.

[4] E. M. Bounds, *Power Through Prayer* (Grand Rapids: Zondervan, 1961), p. 37.

[5] F. L. Cross, ed., "Lutheranism," *The Oxford Dictionary of the Christian Church* (London: Oxford University Press, 1958). See also "Pietism."

[6] Bounds, p. 48.

[7] Thad Rutter, Jr., *Where the Heart Longs to Go* (Nashville: Upper Room Books, 1998), pp. 17, 18ff.

Chapter 2

Worship: Gateway to Communion

"I need to express myself more in worship. I feel closer to God when I do."

"I have learned to come before God's presence with fullness of joy and humble adoration."

—FELLOW SPIRITUAL PILGRIMS

I first "caught" the real spirit of the spiritual disciplines through worship. As I stood in the back of a darkened college church during a student-led worship, three girls led the worship chorus, "I Love You, Lord." Their faces shown as from their hearts they expressed their feelings in song: "I love You, Lord, and I lift my voice to worship You, O my soul, rejoice!" In their joyful expression of personal devotion suddenly everything made sense for me. Worship became more than a liturgy or order of service, and song became more than "preliminaries." These young women were reaching out to express love and devotion to God and inviting us to join them. That act had to be at the core of the spiritual life. What my heart learned that evening became something my mind then pursued. I became convinced that worship is the central priority of God's people. It is at the heart of what He is calling us to do today. And it is the foundation of everything else that He wants to build into our lives.

For many conservative and evangelical Christians the center of life is evangelism or mission. But John Piper makes it clear that there is something more basic:

"Missions is not the ultimate goal of the church. Worship is. Missions exist because worship doesn't. Worship is ultimate, not missions, because God is ultimate, not man. When this age is over, and the countless millions of the redeemed fall on their faces before the throne of God, missions will be no more. It is a temporary necessity. But worship abides forever.

"Worship, therefore, is the fuel and goal in missions."[1]

The Bible and Worship

For Christians, however, worship is central not because Jon Dybdahl experienced it or John Piper writes about it, but because the Bible makes it so. Worship is the predominant activity of believers and the natural response when the awesome loving God of the universe manifests Himself. While biblical instances of worship are sometimes difficult to define, Scripture has at least 400 examples.

But even more than sheer numbers, the call to worship is the most basic command in Scripture. When an expert in religious law asks Jesus, "What is the greatest commandment in the law?" He gives a clear answer.[2] First and foremost, He declares, "You are to love God with all your heart, soul, and mind. Then second, you are to love your neighbor as yourself." According to Jesus, the whole Old Testament hangs on these two commands, because the law and the prophets are the two major sections of that sacred collection.

What does it mean to love God? I have heard it said that you show your love to God by loving other people. That can't be the whole answer, because it turns the first commandment into the second one! While loving God should lead to loving one's neighbor, it has to be more than that.

Scripture makes it clear that you love God by worshipping Him. The two great acts of God in the Old Testament that tower above the biblical landscape are His creation of the world and His deliverance of Israel from Egyptian slavery. Both show God's love and concern for the world and form the reason for all worship. Creation and redemption call forth worship as a loving response to these actions. Since God has created and redeemed us, we ought not only to worship Him, but also to love our neighbors, who also are objects of His love. No wonder Jesus declares that all the Old Testament hangs on these two "commandments." The starting point, however, always is the worship response to God's actions—both large and small—in our lives. We must love/worship Him with all of our hearts and souls.

The centrality of worship also becomes clear as we look at the Ten Commandments personally engraved by God on tablets of stone. Those 10 "words" or commands formed the heart of God's covenant agreement with Israel, and the punishment for breaking them was death. Christianity has a long tradition of connecting the Ten Commandments with the two commandments to love in Matthew 22.[3] Commandments 1-4 define love to God, and commandments 6-10, which admonish us to refrain from stealing, murder, adultery, etc., describe the reality of love to neighbor.

A close look at those first four commandments reveals that they *all* deal with worship. They safeguard worship of Israel's God. Not only that, but the preface in Exodus 20:2 gives the basis or reason for true worship—Yahweh God is the one who has delivered Israel from Egyptian slavery. All calls to true worship stem from the convicting power of that truth about God's redemption.

The first commandment states: "You shall have no other gods before me" (Ex. 20:3). In a world that believed in a multitude of gods and polytheism was rampant, God summoned Israel to "have" or worship only the Redeemer God Yahweh. The commandment does not specifically or implicitly deny the existence of other deities, but simply says that we should not worship them. They are not worthy of the adoration reserved only for the delivering God of the Exodus.

The second commandment forbids the making or worshipping of idols (verses 4-6). Since worship of the idols of other gods would already be covered by the first commandment, the real essence of the second commandment would be the forbidding of the use of images of the true God in worship. Israel was to avoid the worship methods of the surrounding peoples—who made wide use of idols. Idols lessen God by capturing or localizing Him. He is too big and too universal to be limited to a humanly made representation. Those who worship Him can do so any place at any time without dependence on a material representation.

The third commandment forbids taking God's name "in vain" (verse 7, KJV) or misusing it (verse 7). Traditionally many Christians have interpreted the passage as speaking against what we call "swearing" or profanity. Many understand it to mean the use of God's name to curse someone else, or the voicing of inappropriate expletives when we are angry or hurt. No Israelite who valued his life would have even thought of doing such a thing. In later times God's people came to consider His name as so holy that they could never utter it, even in worship. What the passage refers to is using God's name to support one's own words or promises by an oath, such as "I swear by the name of the Most High that I did not steal your lamb." We bring disrespect to God and fail to worship Him when we use Him to back up our words that may or may not be true. Such a concept lies behind Jesus' words in Matthew 5:34-37: "Do not swear at all. . . . Simply let your 'Yes' be 'Yes' and your 'No,' 'No.'" Using God to support our human schemes is failing to give proper worship to Him.

The fourth commandment, Exodus 20:8-11 (see also Deut. 5:12-15), speaks of keeping the Sabbath holy in order to remember God as Creator and Savior from Egyptian slavery. It sets aside time to remember Him. Love requires opportunities for remembrance and thus is part of worship. The fourth commandment safeguards that time of love and worship.

Worship is not only the predominant activity of believers in the Bible and the core of our response to God—it is even a preoccupation in heaven. The book of Revelation graphically pictures a divine realm in which praise has a central place. Four living creatures praise God (Rev. 4:8) as do the 24 elders (verses 10, 11) and an immeasurable host of angels (Rev. 5:11, 12). The chorus of praise songs bursts forth from "every creature in heaven and on earth and under the earth and on the sea, and all that is in them" (verse 13). For the saved believer, praise flows joyfully with a *loud* voice in the courts of heaven (Rev. 7:9, 10).

Why does the Bible identify worship as central to human existence? Why does it call for its careful safeguarding? Why do God's creatures do it not only here but in heaven?

The answer is a simple one. It is that worship shows we understand God's free grace. When we earn something, we do not worship the giver. After all, we *deserve* what we have received. When I get my salary, I do not worship the one signing my check, because I've worked for that money. The issuing of the check is the treasurer just doing his job. Rather, worship is so central because it vividly demonstrates a response to something *undeserved*. God's rescue of Israel did not result from their merit. His deliverance of us from sin does not have its basis on our goodness. There is no way we deserved the grace that we received and no way that we can repay it. The only response we can make is worship as we acknowledge and clearly realize the tremendous love and grace that we have received. To fail to worship is to misunderstand or ignore grace, the core of Christian belief.

What Worship Is (and Is Not)

We may define worship first of all, as a *response* to God's presence and/or action. Worship, then, sees Him as our primary audience, one whom we believe sees our reaching out to Him in praise. While this response can be personal and happen in my private prayer closet, often it will be corporate and take place as a group of believers together seek Him in joy.

Second, worship is a *wholistic* response in which our entire being reaches out. Matthew 22:37, 38 calls on us to love God with all our heart and soul and mind. When that happens, the body is involved as well. Worship, then, includes more than just the cognitive, intellectual reasoning processes. All we are—including body, mind, emotions, will, and spirit—is involved.

Third, worship assumes real *divine-human interchange.* God sees and responds to worship, and the worshipper knows that God is there and basks in His presence. Just as we delight in being in a place where others cherish and love us, so God joyfully shows up where He is worshipped. True worship then feeds itself. As praise begins and the interchange commences, God's presence enters that worship, which in turn intensifies the presence and the worship. It is a far cry from the formal "worship" found in many churches.

One of the problems with worship is that it has become a word used for many things that are not really worship. I see at least four common false models of worship. The first three can operate either corporately or individually.

The first false model is that of the classroom. It views worship as learning. In either our private devotions or church gathering we evaluate what goes on by how much knowledge we acquire. Church becomes a lecture hall, and personal study becomes God's homework. Study is vital, but it is not worship. What study should be is a *prelude to* worship. Knowledge of God leads to worship, and further study should give birth to even more fervent and meaningful worship.

The second false model is that of the evangelistic tent. It regards corporate religious services as a place of proclamation that invites sinners to accept Jesus. Private devotions are to convert or perhaps prepare one to share their faith with others. Again, evangelism itself is not wrong, but it is not worship. Rather, evangelism should be the *result of* worship. Meeting God in worship should inspire and empower us to invite others into the joy of worship.

The third false model is that of the psychologist's couch. This approach uses worship or private adoration as an occasion in which God meets emotional and psychological needs. The sermon is a kind of mass counseling and private prayer is do-it-yourself therapy. One cannot doubt that true religion helps heal people emotionally. But if worship sets out initially to do that, something is not right. I believe that inner emotional healing often takes place as a result of worship. As we admit our unworthiness and celebrate God's grace to us in worship, we are blessed, but it is a derived serendipitous fruit of worship, not the essence of what worship is.

The fourth false model is that of a spectator sport. For many, corporate worship is watching the professionals perform. We evaluate them. If they do well, we cheer, and if they do poorly, we criticize. We in the pew "pay" them to perform and want them to do worship well. Such a model is tragically wrong. Our place in corporate worship is to be *participant,* not spectator.

For me, worship happens only as I join in and actively participate in the worship itself. God is calling us today to return both privately and corporately to real worship. It must become our priority. Next I will outline some biblical teachings on worship and then seek to make some practical suggestions as to how we might revolutionize our own private worship and then be agents of God's renewal of worship in His corporate body, the church.

Bible Words for Worship

The Bible has a rich vocabulary in regard to worship, probably fuller than that concerning any other concept. English stretches to do it justice. Words include "reverence," "glorify," "honor," "praise" (four different Hebrew words), "magnify," "bow down," "fear," "bless," "extol," "adore," "give thanks," and we could go on. Human language and concepts find themselves taxed to the limit when the worthiness of God is the subject of expression.

In the Old Testament the most common word for worship is the verb *šachah.* Used more than 150 times, it has as its basic meaning "to prostrate oneself, bow down deeply, or do homage." The Greek equivalent is "*proskuneo,*" which comes from the word that means literally "to kiss toward." Often when people sought to show reverence to someone higher, they would stoop and/or prostrate themselves and kiss the ground or a proffered foot or hand, ring or scepter. By the time of the New Testament, the word was used exclusively with its object being or supposedly being divine.[4]

The significance of this lies in the fact that for the Bible the root meaning of worship is *physical action.* For the Hebrew, whose worldview closely connected mental processes with physical ones, worship included a mental awe of God and an appropriate physical response. The body and mind go together in worship, and each influences the other.

In fact, Scripture (in particular the Psalms) connects many physical actions directly with worship. They include singing, shouting, dancing, uplifted hands, lifting of the head, kneeling, standing, bowing, prostrating, clapping of hands, bringing offerings, and playing musical instruments. Worship is clearly not intended to be a spectator sport that uses the mind only, but is meant to include the whole person in an active response to God.

When I first began to study this topic, it struck me that I had never prostrated myself before anyone in my life. Early one morning alone in my study I fell on my face and stretched out in awe before God. Something inside of me changed. I felt myself break inside in a way that I had never done before. Since then I have never been the same, and almost every morning now at the start of my devotional time I bow to the ground before the King of kings. I find it puts my life in perspective—I somehow sense who God is and who I am in a way that I cannot experience in any other way. Sometimes I simply maintain that bodily position for a while to let my mind begin to grasp what my body is saying about worship and who God is.

What needs to happen for many Christians—especially conservative, doctrinally oriented ones—is for them to move worship out of the purely rational, cognitive realm. Many such individuals approach worship as a doctrine to accept or believe, not an encounter to experience. Certainly the mind must be part of the worship experience, and people need to know *who* they are worshipping and *why* they seek God. However, if it stops there, we miss something essential. Feeling, passion, zeal, emotion, are all part of worship because the whole person must be part of worship. In John 4:22-24 Jesus calls for true worshippers to worship in spirit and in truth. Some Christian traditions are strong on the truth part but seem to lack spirit. Others may have much spirit and emotion but forget or ignore the value of truth. Jesus wants us to find *both* as we express our love and adoration to Him.

Not only should worship involve the whole person; it must be *participatory*. Corporate worship oriented toward performance misses the mark. The congregation is not the audience for worship—God is. As such, all people should be a part of worship and actively involved. Worship and music leaders are not so much worship leaders as lead worshippers. To truly be lead worshippers, musicians must have a heart for worshipping God, not simply musical ability. They both model worship and invite the gathered people of God to join fully in their worship.

Recognizing the wholistic nature of worship and its participatory nature clarifies the key place of music. Since music directly touches more parts of us than the spoken word, it is important. Properly done, music is participatory.

Many Christian churches have in recent years been involved in music and worship wars. Congregations have debated the appropriateness of certain types of music with great heat. Often reactions split along generational lines.

I do not claim to have all the answers, but several observations may be helpful. It is tragic when battles over music keep people from worship itself. We should always ask the question: Is real worship taking place here? Are people meeting God? If answers seem to be yes, then the music is playing the role it should.

Musical tastes and preferences are always culturally and generationally influenced. What moves my children may not touch me and vice versa. Or what leads a Chinese toward God may not affect me and vice versa. We must be careful that our judgments do not rest solely on what *we* believe is the right way. God can use many types of vehicles for His truth. Even our past history influences the way we perceive various types of music. We must learn to be sensitive to how others see music. Discussions over music should never keep us from using this God-given medium as an effective part of true worship. If there is anything that I hope this chapter does, it is to move people back to the centrality of worship both corporately and privately. Corporate worship all too easily slips back into the learning classroom mold when the center of things becomes a teaching sermon. Worship services should be about worship. People must self-consciously worship, and the one in charge of the service must deliberately lead the congregation into worship. Even the result of the sermon should be a worship response—praise to God for what He has done, awe at His works, or repulsion at our waywardness before Him.

On a personal level, for many people their devotional time centers on a reading of inspirational material or Bible study. Nothing is wrong with such a practice, but again the basic mode becomes the homework cognitive learning model. Devotion time should be at its core worship. Again, even the study must lead to worship. A time of prostration, a time of praise with hands and heart uplifted, a time of listening to music and responding and joining in, a time of singing or playing of musical instruments—such things are all true devotion and worship, not just something preliminary.

Many worship directors cannot truly lead because they have not worshipped personally in preparation beforehand. And many worshippers find corporate worship a challenge because they also have not worshipped personally. A person transformed in their private prayer discovers new life in otherwise unchanged corporate worship. They find something catching, something drawing—yes, even something evangelistic—about corporate worship that takes place in spirit and in truth. When you enter a place where people have a heart for God and are reaching out to Him, you sense it. You find yourself drawn to it and want to be a part of it. Many churches are not evangelistic because, lacking true worship, their sense of God's presence has become only a distant memory, not a present experience.

Practical Steps

How does one begin to understand and experience worship? How can one who lacks true worship find it? I have a few suggestions.

First, reflect on or seek a new experience of the grace, love, and awesomeness of

God. All true worship springs from a sense of whom God is, which then reveals whom we are. Isaiah in his experience recorded in Isaiah 6 offers a model. His vision of the awesomeness and holiness of God drove him to worship and a deep sense of his own uncleanness. This in turn led to a statement of God's forgiveness and cleansing and a divine commissioning. Such a realization about God is not a doctrine or a theology, but a whole person insight that affects all that we are.

Second, deliberately begin to take time personally to act and react in response to the experience of God. For Westerners that may best be done personally. Kneel and thank Him for His goodness. Sing a song or write a poem as an offering for what He has done for you. Stand in awe and bow your head at a sunset or sunrise. Lift your hands and offer Him all you are. Voice out loud your praise. Do whatever comes naturally as you respond fully to Him. Let body and heart and mind work together as you experience Him. Remember that what you are doing is not some preliminary to something else. You are fulfilling the essence, the core of a believer's life. Let your joy and your feelings flow out in praise. You will be surprised by His presence and the response will grow and the presence will deepen. Make worship a major part of your personal private devotional time.

Third, let your new experience of worship transform your corporate experience. One student who studied the topic of worship came back and told how understanding worship itself had transformed her corporate worship experience even though nothing in the actual order of service changed. *She* had been transformed personally, and that had altered her corporate worship. How does this happen? Pause before entering church and thank God for a place where His name can be praised. Ask Him to move in you and in others during the service. Enter the sanctuary with joy, thanking God for inviting you and for another week of life. Look at other parishioners as brothers and sisters in worship and thank God for them. Kneel briefly as you sit down and then start your worship immediately. Participate fully in every part of the service, listening to the prayers and singing the songs from your heart. Do everything as an offering to God. You are there not to *get* a blessing, but to *give* a blessing, having come to bless and to worship God by joining in a corporate worship fest. Not all will know what you are doing, but getting even a few to start joining you will transform the spirit of the service. The worship service will become different even though outwardly it appears to remain the same. And in the end the order of service may itself begin to alter.

As I teach many eager seminary students, some assume that just changing the order of service or the type of music will bring a worship renewal. That is not true. What needs to alter are people's hearts and minds. When people meet God, worship will transform itself naturally. The order of service and music can help facilitate true worship, but having the right heart for worship is still the key.

Conclusion

Humanity's initial true response to God's action and presence was worship. That never ends. The book of Revelation portrays the inhabitants of heaven in worship forever. Many things begin and then end. But worship for true believers never ceases. Shouldn't we heed God's call and start experiencing real worship now? It is one thing that we can enjoy forever.

When we truly worship we begin at a deep level to see God in all His love and glory. The natural next step is to look at ourselves. When Isaiah did that (Isa. 6), he immediately found himself overwhelmed with a keen sense of his sin and unworthiness. Following that sequence, our next chapter deals with the suggestions to help us take the step of serious self-examination and find God's solution to our deep need.

---

[1] John Piper, *Let the Nations Be Glad! The Supremacy of God in Mission* (Grand Rapids: Baker Book House, 1993), p. 11.

[2] Note the whole passage in Matthew 22:34-40 and the parallel in Mark 12:28-31.

[3] See Ex. 20:1-17 and Deut. 5:6-21.

[4] Gerhard Friedrich and Geoffrey W. Bromiley, eds., *Theological Dictionary of the New Testament* (Grand Rapids: Eerdmans, 1968), Vol. VI, pp. 758-766.

Chapter 3

Repentance, Confession, and Forgiveness

"He [God] likes music, hot tubs, journals, prostrate prayers, bicycling, hot baths, raised hands, and some Bible reading (although not required like seminary). I also learned that God likes honest people."

"I realized that the vast majority of my actions are motivated by very selfish motives, and I am referring to all types of actions that could be considered pious or evil."

—Fellow Spiritual Pilgrims

Worship is the first doorway to the spiritual disciplines, because it makes a statement about who God is. Repentance, confession, and forgiveness form the second doorway into the disciplines, because they clarify whom we are. The other disciplines are predicated on these two foundations. If a person lacks a clear understanding of the nature of God and the human condition, it is impossible for the other disciplines to function as they should. The two doorway spiritual disciplines thus lay an essential foundation for all that follows. If you get them right, it is much easier for all else to come in proper order.

The Bible and Repentance

Repentance is the core of Jesus' teaching and the Bible. Building on John the Baptist's summons to repent (Matt. 3:2; Mark 1:4; Luke 3:3),

Jesus centered His early preaching on a similar call. The Gospel writers Matthew (Matt. 4:17), Mark (Mark 1:15), and Luke (Luke 5:32; 13:3, 5) testify that Jesus made repentance a cornerstone of His message. When Jesus sent out the 12 disciples to minister, their fundamental preaching message was the same (Mark 6:12). Jesus and His disciples healed the sick and cast out demons, but such acts sought to lead people to repentance. Acts 2:37, 38 makes repentance the central issue in the first recorded post-resurrection Christian sermon. It was the key to early Christian teaching (Acts 3:17-20). Paul the evangelist understood that in an earlier era repentance may not have been necessary, but now God "commands all people everywhere to repent" (Acts 17:30). The older testament as well portrays a need for human repentance, something especially evident in the prophets (see, for example, Isaiah 31:6; 59:20; Jeremiah 3:7-14; 18:8; 26:3; Ezekiel 14:6; 18:30-32; 33:11-19). Some miss this emphasis, for the Old Testament often expresses it as a "turning," which is a literal translation of the Hebrew word *shub*. God through all time has been interested in calling people to turn (or to return or turn again) to Him.

What does it mean to repent? As already stated, in the Hebrew Old Testament "repent" means to turn or return. The New Testament Greek equivalent word is "metanoia," meaning a change of mind. The core concept is of a shift of basic orientation. You are headed in one direction but turn to move in another. Once you looked at things from one viewpoint, but now you see from a whole new perspective.

To repent implies that the previous mind-set is faulty. Traditionally Christians have called the old outlook "sin." Often, however, they misunderstand the word. To grasp more clearly what is going on, it is helpful to differentiate between *sins* and *sin*. Sins refer to specific behavioral problems, whether great or small. Lying, cheating, and sexual immortality are examples. But sin involves the basic separation or alienation between God and humanity. That underlying broken relationship gives rise to all the behavioral challenges (sins).

A good illustration of how it works is to compare it with weeds in the garden. I grew up in California, and my mom often had me hoeing the garden. In my haste to finish the task I often chopped off the visible leafy part of the weeds, leaving the root buried out of sight.

Unfortunately, the root soon produced new leaves and an even tougher stem. The root sin is what gives rise to the weeds (sins). You can chop off sins, but unless you deal with sin, you have not solved the problem.

Such an illustration not only helps us define sin and sins, but points out a common difficulty. In decades of dealing with people in spiritual counseling, I have seen individuals time and again repeatedly confess sins while being unable or unwilling to repent of sin, or they remain blind to sin in their lives. Some may confess overeating or failure to attend church but at the same time insist on following their own direction in life, not God's. They may admit to Him their over indulgences in doughnuts but continue to harbor deep long-term anger at their mother. While such confession of specific sins is not wrong, we must focus on the core issue of who has our fundamental allegiance. In Scripture repentance in a majority of cases deals with life orientation. Thus God repeatedly calls Israel back to allegiance to Him rather than to foreign gods. As we read passages such as Isaiah 31:6, Jeremiah 3:7-14, and Hosea 11, it becomes clear that God desperately longs for the (re)turn (repentance) of His people from their flirtation with other deities. John the Baptist urges hearers to "bear fruits that befit repentance" (Luke 3:8, RSV), which seems obviously to mean that specific acts ("fruits") must demonstrate the basic orientation change that repentance refers to. But preoccupation with specific acts and their admission does not deal with the heart of the repentance issue. God is calling for a core transformation in life attitude, one that widely affects behavior in all areas.

Repentance and confession go together and seem by their very nature to imply each other. If one repents or changes life orientation, it involves a tacit admission (confession) that the old way was inferior. And if one acknowledges that life in the past was wrong or inferior (confession), the natural connotation would be that a change (repentance) would be a good thing. The two thus dance in complementary fashion on the stage of life.

The Challenge of Practicing Repentance

While this may all sound simple and straightforward, in actual practice it is—if done properly—challenging. The process is difficult and can be excruciatingly painful. As a pastor and teacher I continually meet people who will try to escape true repentance and confession by any means possible, because it is so costly. Often the avoidance is not even conscious. Like Adam and Eve, who hid in the garden to avoid God's visit (Gen. 3:8), people still "hide out" from Him because a true encounter in repentance and confession is just too hard.

Such avoidance and "hiding out" happens in a variety of ways. One takes place *by focusing repentance on the small things*—especially those dealing with behaviors. Some can begin to believe that they have cared for repentance by concentrating on a few bad habits. By doing this, they assume that they can safely avoid having to deal with the major life orientation that Jesus is concerned about.

Others try *pretense* as a means to escape. They attempt to hide their sin and need from themselves and those around them by acting as if nothing happened. The attempt fails, because at the core of their being they know there remains a problem. While they are lying to themselves, they still know that they can't really deceive God.

Still others try to *deny their sin.* Immorality becomes love, pursuit of riches becomes good stewardship, shutting God out of the decision-making process is clear, rational thinking, and lying becomes politeness. Such a path quickly leads to even greater denial, self-deception, and sins.

Many seek to avoid repentance *by excusing their problem.* They find ways to rationalize and lessen its seriousness, or they shift blame to some person or event in the past. Such individuals play the victim and escape personal responsibility. They do everything possible to avoid reality even though the lie they live will inevitably lead to disillusionment.

Honesty (Confession) Pays

The core value that God is desperately seeking here is honesty. We must admit what we have done and acknowledge a better way. All of us must recognize that we are tempted to remain what M. Scott Peck calls "people of the lie."[1] Somehow we must finally admit that focusing on the trivial, existing on pretense and denial, and making excuses for what we do are all counterproductive. Such things ultimately destroy soul and body. Eating away at our spirit and damaging our psyche, they turn out to be a very heavy burden to bear.

But there is good news. The fruit of real repentance and confession is full, true joy. Let me explain. The bliss of honesty and forgiveness more than matches the pain of repentance.

Psychological research has amply demonstrated that openness and honesty about our situation and feelings is highly beneficial. James Pennebaker in his book *Opening Up*[2] explains in detail his research dealing with the benefits of expressing our deepest thoughts and feelings. In both the initial chapter of the book and the next-to-concluding chapter, he ties his work directly to religions that support confession. According to Pennebaker, actually holding back or inhibiting our thoughts and feelings is hard work and eventually undermines the body's defenses and weakens the immune system.[3] In fact, college graduates who simply wrote out their "confession" visited the health clinic at half the rate of those who had not done so.[4] Opening up not only helps our physical health but is psychologically beneficial. Pennebaker even found that it assisted people to find jobs after getting laid off.[5]

In other words, what the Bible describes as a healthy spirituality turns out to be literally "healthful" in many other areas. The honesty that underlies true repentance and confession leads not only to spiritual health but physical, psychological, and relational health as well.

Forgiveness

But that is not all. The Bible teaches that the result of repentance and confession is forgiveness. John the Baptist's baptism of repentance had a purpose. It was literally "for the forgiveness of sins" (Mark 1:4; Luke 3:3). The account of the first post-Resurrection Christian sermon in Acts 2:38 makes clear that the same thing is true for Christians. Peter tells his hearers that they should repent and be baptized "for the forgiveness of your sins." Scripture is quite specific that God is a sin-forgiving Deity, and that the forgiveness experience becomes a reality when we admit our need for it.

Perhaps the most well-known passage that Christians use is 1 John 1:9: "If we confess our sins, he is faithful and just and will forgive our sins and purify us from all unrighteousness." Repenters and confessors take heart!

Our problem is that for many, forgiveness is a doctrine, and thus they have little understanding of the actual process and dynamics involved. Few of us actually think about forgiveness in any depth. Here we want at least to begin by asking what forgiveness is (and is not) and the different kinds of forgiveness that exist. Then we need to consider what the experience of forgiveness consists of.

The Old Testament most often conveys forgiveness by Hebrew words that mean "send away" or "cover."[6] The New Testament generally uses "send away," but it also employs "loose," "be gracious to," and "pass over." Perhaps a good modern English word to employ would be "release."

I have focused on the literal meanings of the various words because they are significant. In many cases people have placed far too much theological and rational weight on them, particularly as it relates to forgiving other people. Consider the following points.

Forgiving does not mean forgetting. To "release" or "send away" something does not suggest an inability to remember it. God may be able to choose to forget, but humans tend to remember even more the things they try to shove out of their thoughts. To forgive another does not require amnesia.

Forgiving does not mean condoning. Many victims of crime do not want to forgive, because they feel that such action would condone or excuse the heinous acts of the perpetrator. Forgiveness need not lessen our sense of outrage about a terrible deed. To release something does not lessen the guilt of the wrongdoer. God's forgiveness of our sin does not approve of our action or lessen His holiness and righteousness.

Forgiving does not mean pardoning. While in some cases, such as God's forgiveness of sin, the ultimate punishment may be waived, in human-to-human relationships forgiveness does not demand that the forgiver must advocate the release of the criminal from all punishment. Even in God's forgiveness, the physical effects of, for instance, the abuse of one's body may still linger. Forgiveness does not mean canceling or negating punishments or results.

Forgiving does not necessarily lead to reconciliation. In many cases, we should attempt reconciliation, but in some cases one party or the other is not interested. You don't have to be friends with your daughter's abuser. God wants to reconcile with us, but some humans may not!

Back to our main point—forgiveness is to release or send away. What all that means in each case may vary. Actually, God's forgiveness is deeper than human forgiveness. In some cases human forgiveness may mean simply not hanging on to or obsessing about the event, and letting God work on making whatever adjustments to the situation as He sees fit.

It seems in fact that there exists *at least five different kinds of forgiveness.* First is God's forgiveness of persons, the most commonly spoken of type by Christians. Second is forgiveness by others. Both are passive types of forgiveness that we need to receive.

The third type of forgiveness is that of persons toward God. We are not saying here that God did anything wrong and needs to be forgiven, but rather that many people blame Him for all kinds of unpleasant events in their life. Forgiveness to God means that we give up trying to charge Him with responsibility and deal then with the situation in a more productive manner. The fourth type of forgiveness focuses on those who have wronged us. Both of these types of forgiveness are in the active mode and relate to our response to perceived sins against us. We will discuss the fourth type of forgiveness in depth shortly. The fifth type of forgiveness deals with our forgiving ourselves. While such self-forgiveness may seem strange at first, it is vital to our spiritual and psychological health. We must all have sometime heard a friend say, "I can never forgive myself for . . ." The point is that to be whole we must find a way to do the very thing we claim that we can never do.

Forgiving Others

Christians have always taught that forgiving others was a part of their faith. In part it goes back to Jesus words at His own crucifixion: "Father, forgive them; for they know not what they do" (Luke 23:34, KJV). We assume that if Jesus is asking God to forgive, then He has already done so Himself. The whole issue is enshrined in the Lord's Prayer (Matt. 6:14, 15; Luke 11:2-4). Matthew in particular seems to make God's forgiveness of us contingent on our willingness to forgive others: "But if you do not forgive men their trespasses, neither will your Father forgive your trespasses" (Matt. 6:15, RSV).

Some have seen this as a straightforward statement that a condition for God's forgiveness is forgiveness offered to others. While this may be partially true, I believe that a much deeper dynamic is going on here. It is a law of the human mind that we cannot receive what we refuse to offer. Almost as if we have a built-in fairness gene, we cannot know God's forgiveness in a deep experiential sense if we have not offered it to others. We come right up to that acceptance of forgiveness, and as we're ready to receive it that "fairness gene" kicks in. "You can't forgive your neighbor," it tells us, "and if that is true, God can never forgive you." Here we enter the heart of why many cannot accept at a deep level God's forgiveness of their sins.

The truth of Matthew's version of the Lord's Prayer is thus not that God has arbitrarily said "If you don't forgive others, you'll never be forgiven," but that He created our human nature to monitor fairness, and it won't let anything violate that inner sense.

One could go on to say that difficulty in actualizing even one of the types of forgiveness hampers a full experience of all the others as well. Christians need to recognize that the topic of repentance, confession, and forgiveness is receiving massive new attention in the world of social sciences. In fact, "social scientists are discovering that forgiveness may help lead to victims' emotional and even physical healing and wholeness."[7]

Certainly if the world at large is realizing the significance of this fact, Christians should show renewed interest not simply in the theology but also the experience and practice of these crucial elements.

How to Practice Repentance and Forgiveness

Now we must answer several key questions and then discuss how to practice these key disciplines. The first question is How does one enter this powerful experience? Repentance, confession, and forgiveness all come because God graciously provides for them. They "work" because He ordained that they heal our lives. Not only does God wish that "all should reach repentance" (2 Peter 3:9, RSV), but even only one repentant sinner brings joy to heaven (Luke 15:7). One major purpose of His kindness has as its aim to lead us to repentance (Rom. 2:4). God often employs a renewed sense of His great grace and matchless love to motivate us toward repentance.

Such an experience can come on the heels of worship as it did for Isaiah. When in vision he saw God in all His glory (Isa. 6:1-3), it drove him to declare, "Woe is me! I am lost, for I am a man of unclean lips" (verse 5, NRSV). The prophet's confession led him to communion with

God and a life of service. Isaiah's deep need for cleansing brought him and continues to bring us to the great divine cleanser of sin, who grants forgiveness joyfully to all repenters and confessors.

The second question concerns whether repentance is a one-time experience or an ongoing process or spiritual discipline. While it is clear that many New Testament passages use repentance primarily to speak of the basic change that takes place at the onset of the Christian life, ample evidence indicates that the development of the full dimensions of the experience are ongoing as one lives the Christian life. James 5:16 admonishes us to confess our sins to one another and be healed. Both verb form and context clearly imply that it is a repeatable experience. Luke 17:3, 4 tells us that if others repent, we should forgive them, and if they sin against us seven times in one day but say, "I repent," we must forgive them. Repentance is a continuous Christian style of life.

How then does one apply all of this to the Christian walk? First, we must carefully examine how one begins the Christian life. Many learn repentance, confession, and forgiveness as Christian beliefs. They are something a believer assents to. But ideally all three things should also be presented as an experience that Christians are blessed to take part in and then practice in their lives as an ongoing and developing growth experience. One could even create a worksheet or "homework" paper in which new believers take time to in quietness ask God what repentance means to them in a general attitude and life-orientation way and then in specific life behaviors.

An honored tradition in many Protestant groups has prospective church members appearing before members of the church family and giving a statement of their Christian experience. Repentance, confession, and forgiveness would be a key part of that. Sadly, many churches no longer do this. While the public nature of such an event may be problematic, certainly the core concept is a valid one.

Once believers have begun a serious Christian life in this way, such principles should continue to be a part of Christian spirituality and devotional practice. I suggest that monthly and yearly the church should set aside a special time for each member to examine their lives. It could well provide the context of a spiritual retreat. Daily, as a regular practice, we need to ask how we are doing in the specific areas in which we find ourselves challenged in our spiritual journey. Is Jesus the Lord of our life in each instance? This should lead to confession of sin not as a form, but as a serious and daily reality check. It then serves as a doorway to the other disciplines of spiritual communion, such as prayer, journaling, and Scripture study.

Most Protestants have traditionally regarded such a daily examen [examination] a private, individual matter. In many cases it can be, but we must come to realize that at times even Scripture suggests that we should involve others. We humans have a tremendous capacity for self-deception and denial—especially when it comes to an objective evaluation of our problems.

At times we can also have doubts about the reality of our forgiveness. Both problems can find their solution involving selected others in the process of repentance, confession, and forgiveness. James 5:16 says: "Confess your sins [the original Greek here is the regular New Testament word for sin, *hamartia*] to one another, and pray for one another, that you may be healed" (RSV). One way we Christians can make this happen is to have a confidential small group who can perform the functions of keeping us honest and assuring us of forgiveness. Eighteenth- and nineteenth-century Methodists in a weekly "class meeting" of about 12 members began with frank discussions of the spiritual condition of each member and how they had done in their struggle with sin. It was a requirement of church membership. Many have seen the loss of this dynamic as one reason Methodism has declined in spiritual power.

If such a group is not available, you can seek out a discreet, mature Christian who can honestly and sympathetically listen to your spiritual challenges. Those of the same gender are best. Encourage them to be honest and to apply the Word of God to your life. Even if you regard yourself a mature Christian, do not consider the concept as irrelevant. Time and again I have seen both new and longtime Christians grow tremendously when they take repentance and forgiveness seriously. I have employed a multipage questionnaire for people to use in their evaluation of such issues. It helps both to focus on key issues and to consider all areas of life.

Conclusion

God promises that those who take confession and repentance seriously and receive and give forgiveness will reap great rewards. I have found that to be true. Wouldn't you like to be one of them?

Seeing God for who He is, worshipping Him and then looking at ourselves leads to repentance and the giving and receiving of forgiveness. Now we are ready to move on and communicate with Him. The core of such communion is prayer and meditation.

We will study these in the next two chapters.

---

[1] M. Scott Peck, *People of the Lie: the Hope for Healing Evil* (New York: Simon and Schuster, 1983).

[2] James W. Pennebaker, *Opening Up*, rev. ed. (New York: Guilford Press, 1997).

[3] *Ibid.*, pp. 2-4.

[4] *Ibid.*, p. 34.

[5] *Ibid.*, pp. 38, 39.

[6] Paul J. Achtemeier, ed., *Harper's Bible Dictionary* (San Franscisco: Harper and Row, 1985), p. 319.

[7] Gary Thomas, "The Forgiveness Factor," *Christianity Today*, Jan. 10, 2000, pp. 38-45.

Chapter 4

Prayer and Meditation I

"Praying has become a necessity in my life now."

"The greatest thing has happened in these devotions that I have in the morning. I have felt the peace of God. I don't really know how to describe it; I would say it is a sense of total abandon, relaxation (not from being sleepy), joy, and love—all from God and all at once."

—Fellow Spiritual Pilgrims

Introduction

Worship has taught us who God is, and in repentance we have discovered who we are. The next step is putting the two understandings together. How can God and humans have interchange? That is the subject of the rest of this book. Christianity teaches that God meant that He and humanity were to be in relationship. Communion of the human and the divine is God's plan, and the way that communion takes place is what we will discuss in this chapter and the ones to follow. We'll begin with the topic of prayer and meditation because it is by far the most common way that the Bible speaks about communion taking place.

Even though this chapter focuses mainly on prayer and the next one on meditation, I have used both words in the title of both chapters, because the words and the spiritual practices connected with them have often been separated too widely. I find that both in the Bible and in practice the two often blend and flow into one another. They have a lot of overlap, and some aspects are difficult to define as to whether they are prayer or meditation. One typical way of differentiating is to say that prayer is verbal while meditation is silent or wordless. But the Bible does portray prayer as at times silent, and meditation in many cases uses words, as we will see in the following chapter.

Prayer in the Bible

Next to worship, prayer is by far the most talked-about religious experience of believers in the Bible. Herbert Lockyer's book *All the Prayers of the Bible* says in its foreword that Scripture contains "no fewer than 650 definite prayers, of which no less than 450 have recorded answers."[1] And this is exclusive of the Psalms, which is a prayer book as well as a songbook.

As one surveys biblical prayers, at least two things stand out beside the fact that prayer is extremely important and common. *First is the tremendous variety we find.* Prayer is central to major corporate events such as the Temple dedication (1 Kings), political/military crises (2 Kings), and times of religious transition (Dan. 9; 10). Personal prayer is appropriate at times of vocational crises (as in Jeremiah) and when one is desperately seeking religious answers during trying times (Habakkuk). Generations of believers continue to find in the book of Psalms prayers that relate to any personal crisis they face, from loss of friends to physical sickness.

Not only did Jesus teach widely on prayer—the Gospels portray Him as a person of prayer, who prays in all kinds of situations. From His 40-day desert temptations (Matt. 4:2; Luke 4:2) to intercession for His disciples (John 17) to a prayer with a desperate question to God (Matt. 27:46), Jesus Himself prayed. In the one place in the Gospels that seems to record a typical 24-hour day of Jesus (Mark 1:21-38), He arises before dawn to seek a solitary place for prayer.

The book of Acts depicts the early church believers as utterly depending on prayer. Acts mentions prayer or praying more than 30 times, and every advance or growth of the church seems to stem from prayer. The apostle Paul usually begins his letters with written prayers and also mentions his own private prayers for the people and churches that he has labored for.

The bottom line is that there seems to be no circumstance in which prayer would be out of place. No group can be too large or too small to pray, and no occasion is inappropriate for prayer.

Second, prayer is a time for complete honesty. There is no feeling or emotion that cannot be expressed in prayer. People pray when they are happy and celebrating and when they are sad and depressed. People pray even when they are cynical or angry.

Lack of understanding here often becomes a major barrier to prayer for many people. Prayer seems contrived and artificial to them because they have been taught to "talk nice" to God. Any sense of questioning, frustration, or anger is out of bounds. But such a perspective of prayer is not the biblical/Christian view. Read the prayers of Jeremiah, who boldly expresses his frustration to God (Jer. 12:1ff.; 20:14ff.). Meditate on Habakkuk's persistent theological questioning of God (1:1ff.). Contemplate the Psalms and notice the brutal honesty expressed even to the point of advocating violence on enemies (Ps. 2:9; 137:9). Hear Jesus' agonizing question to God from the cross: "My God, my God, why have you forsaken me?" (Matt. 27:46). If you take this seriously, you will feel a new freedom to pray honestly and openly and authentically.

People want to hear such prayer. Several years ago a good friend died of cancer. At that time she was mothering her two teenage daughters and was a pillar of the church and community. I had prayed specifically for her healing, as had many others. If anyone deserved God's healing, it seemed to us that she did. Her death not only saddened us deeply but aroused age-old questions about God. The family asked me to give a prayer during her memorial service, one attended by hundreds of people. After serious thought I decided to pray my real feelings. I spoke openly about my questions about why this had happened, but concluded by saying that in spite of my frustration with God there was no place else to turn. I have never received so many comments on a prayer. Person after person said I had expressed their hidden heart questions. I now encourage all I counsel not to begin praying unless they can pray honestly.

Defining Prayer

How can we define the universal phenomenon of prayer?

I suggest that prayer is *"reaching out to share with God as Friend and Lord."* The definition has three essential elements. *First, prayer involves intention and choice.* That is the reason for the words "reaching out." Prayer is a decision that we can enter into or choose not to. God doesn't force us to pray—we decide to.

Second, I deliberately use the word "share" because it can imply both speaking and listening, both silence and words as well as action. Definitions that suggest prayer as mainly talk to God are only partial. Thus prayer includes the whole spectrum of actions that people perform as they communicate with each other.

Third, prayer reaches out to God through Jesus—recognizing Him as both Lord and Friend. The call here is for balance. While the Bible speaks about friendship with God, we cannot forget that He is also Lord of lords and King of the universe. We must always strongly affirm Jesus both as friend and as ruler of the universe and all heavenly and earthly powers. If either concept were to overwhelm or cancel out the other, the biblical tension would be lost. Such tension is a healthy one. In prayer when we worship and seek to know God's will for our lives, we look to Him as Lord. When we share our intimate problems and desires, we come as friends, believing that as a loving Lord He will act on our behalf.

Christian prayer, when entered into in a regular, formal sense, has four key elements—all beginning with the letter *a.*

The first is *address.* Whom do we speak to when we pray? We are addressing the God of our Lord Jesus Christ. Here is what makes prayer Christian. Instead of encountering, for example, the impersonal God of the Hindu philosopher, we are privileged to speak to the God of the Bible, who has specifically instructed us in the New Testament to call Him Father. Much has been made about the New Testament use of the word "abba" on the lips of Jesus. Although sometimes popularly translated "daddy," both children and adults did employ it when speaking to their fathers. If we take the Gospels seriously, we find evidence that Jesus used "abba" in prayer (see, for example, Mark 14:36) to address God. It undoubtedly lies behind the use of the word "father" in the Lord's Prayer (Matt. 6:9; Luke 11:2). Such use was not common in that day and probably represents a unique contribution of Jesus. For Jews who reverenced God's name so highly that they set up elaborate procedures not to blaspheme it, Jesus' use is unprecedented. Many who have been raised praying Christian prayers have no sense of what it meant for a first-century Jew to use these words. In Jesus' day it was the custom that various teachers, rabbis, or gurus gave their disciples a prayer to pray that summarized and perhaps epitomized the rabbi's teaching. It seems clear in Luke 11 that John the Baptist had done that and that Jesus' disciples were asking him to do the same (Luke 11:1). The fact that He employed the address "father" or "our father" at the beginning of the prayer speaks clearly to us that this specific address is a significant part of Christian theology and prayer. Even Jews and Muslims, religious cousins of Christians, do not employ such terminology. To pray "Abba, Father" speaks volumes to what Jesus tells us about God and the familial core of Christian faith. Christians who utter this word in prayer should revel in the glory and wonder of it. One could, in fact, pray simply "Abba, Abba" and have prayed well as a Christian.

In a world increasingly sensitive to sexism and gender prejudice, please remember that what the Bible says or what I have written is not meant to deal with gender issues. God is Mother as well as Father in Christian theology,[2] and thus the use of this word seeks to speak to intimacy and care rather than the gender of the parent referred to. We are all children of a divine heavenly Parent who wraps up in one being the caring elements of both human parents.

Second, after addressing God, we *adore*. We come with worship, praise, and thanksgiving for all that we have received from His hand. As we "enter his gates with thanksgiving and his courts with praise" (Ps. 100:4) we recognize clearly what God has done for us and who He is.

Third, we *ask*. Unfortunately for some, this makes up the main part of the prayer. On the other hand, we must remember that the biblical model does include petition as part of prayer. Certainly, sincere believers should share their needs with God. In such asking we may include our own requests, but a large part of asking should be intercessory prayer on behalf of others. While requests may be spiritual, they need not leave out physical needs. After all, the Lord's Prayer does include a petition for "daily bread."

Fourth, we close our prayer by singling out our *advocate*. Who is going to make this prayer effectual? How will it be offered to God? Who is the one who gives our prayer authority? For the Christian, that is Jesus. Christ tells His disciples, "Whatever you ask in my name, I will do it, that the Father may be glorified in the Son. If you ask anything in my name, I will do it" (John 14:13, 14, RSV). Again, Jesus declares in John's Gospel: "If you ask anything of the Father, he will give it to you in my name. Hitherto you have asked nothing in my name; ask and you will receive, that your joy may be full" (John 16:23, 24, RSV). Clearly, to request in Jesus' name is vital.

What this means is that because of what Jesus did and who He is, we as Christians pray in a new way. We have an advocate who empowers our prayers. Our prayers go to God in the name and power of a risen Lord.

What is unique about Christian prayer is *not* that we offer praise to the deity and/or that we make petitions. Other religions do the same in prayer. What is special is how we address God (in familiar, intimate, family terms) and the powerful, authoritative, caring advocate in whose name we present the prayer. Those two parts of prayer that we most often hastily pass over and perhaps at times not even utter are the core essence of truly Christian prayers. They give the setting and context for our praise and petition and are the reason we expect God to respond.

How to Pray

When speaking to people about their challenges in praying, I discover many who find prayer extremely boring. They feel that it is either a duty to pray or that they had better pray or God will reject them. But the resulting prayer is unsatisfactory. I have two suggestions in such an instance.

First, I tell such individuals to pray as they can (authentically), not as they can't (artificially). In other words, start prayer right where you are rather than pretending to be or do something you aren't. This is where honesty comes in. If you are bored, tell God. "I'm bored and I have a very hard time making meaning out of prayer. Can You help me? What should I do?" If you are not even sure you believe in prayer, acknowledge it: "I'm not sure You're even there or are even able to answer, but this is my attempt to reach out. Are You there? How do I contact You and You me?" If you are a longtime Christian and prayer has lost its punch, tell God exactly where you are, and ask Him to help change your situation. Many find this step to authenticity and honesty a breath of fresh air that jump-starts prayer again for them.

The second suggestion I have is to find some new ways to pray that can give you additional paths to commune and communicate with the King of the universe. I will start you with seven suggestions to open more windows on prayer.

1. *Setting the Stage.* Picture two ways of eating spaghetti. In the first scenario you come into the house wearing your grubbies after working in the yard. Time is short, so you grab a plastic container of pasta. Opening a jar of tomato sauce, you pour it on top of the pasta. You wolf down the spaghetti while standing in the kitchen and then rush on to your next task. Scenario two involves a sit-down romantic dinner. The dining room table is set with the best china and silver you have. Warm spaghetti is elegantly served in the best serving bowl. Lights are dimmed, and soft music plays in the background. You have dressed in your finest for the occasion. Time stands still for a special moment of meeting with someone treasured.

In both scenarios the spaghetti has the same food value and number of calories, but the experience is entirely different. I am not claiming that we can call on God only when we are well dressed and the table is set. Short prayers during the day are helpful in any context. Rather, what I am saying is that the setting really matters when we take time for serious prayer and devotion.

Jesus evidently found solitary places helped in His prayer life (see, for example, Mark 1:35; 6:45, 46). Many employ a special room or chair to help get them in the right attitude. I know one woman who creates her special setting by first opening the door to let God into the room before she begins to pray. Others use a special prayer rug or kneeling bench. Some may light a candle or dim the lights. Perhaps a memento of a special experience with God will help you establish a personal setting. Even special scents can help. The Israelite sanctuary in the center of the camp where God manifested His presence was known for its special sweet aroma. It came from a unique anointing oil blended by a perfumer (Ex. 30:22-38). The sanctuary in all its parts, as well as the priests, was anointed with "God's perfume." People outside could not, on the pain of punishment, use the same recipe. The specific aroma triggered in God's people a sense of His nearness. We must find all the ways we can to create in our lives places of "sweet smell" that elicit for us a sense of divine presence. When we enter such a place, we have already begun to pray, because we have reached out to God.

2. Music and Singing. Many do not realize how many sacred songs are or could be prayers. The songbook of Scripture, the Psalms, is also its prayer book. For many Christians music expresses the most moving part of their faith. While most corporate Christian worship includes music, many fail to use it in their prayer life. The possibilities range from soothing background music for inspirational reading to the memorizing and/or personal singing of songs or hymns during a devotional time. My wife feels closest to God when she sits at the piano and plays and sings religious songs that speak to her soul. When done for Jesus and to Jesus, it is definitely prayer. During a particularly dry time in my spiritual life both formal prayer and study seemed to do nothing for me, but what fed my soul and led me to divine communion was listening in a quiet basement room to Jesus songs and then, as the Spirit led, singing and or responding in ways that the music suggested—kneeling, raising hands, and prostrating myself. Such practices can be endlessly adapted to the specific needs and temperament of the one praying. Experiment with this way of prayer if it seems attractive to you.

3. Journaling. In a later chapter I will say more about journaling in general, but I must here mention it specifically in relationship to prayer for at least two reasons.

First, many people find it very helpful to write prayers or letters to God. I can remember a woman coming to me in tears after I gave a lecture on journaling. She shared how for a number of years her practice of writing her prayers in the form of letters to God had blessed her spiritual life. Someone, however, had told her that this wasn't praying and that she should kneel, close her eyes, and speak her prayers if she really wanted to pray. Now she thanked me profusely for giving her permission to write her prayers and for affirming the fact that what she had been doing was, in fact, prayer.

Second, I personally find writing in a journal one of the best ways to listen to God, an oft-neglected key aspect of prayer. I can still remember the first time that I tried this. I'm not sure why I was so hesitant and fearful about asking God to speak. My thought was *What if He asks me to do something weird?* After delaying for weeks, I finally one morning after a time of worship sat down with pencil and paper, asked for God's special presence, and said, "What do you want to say to me?" The first thing I heard was my name. "Jon, Jon, you are My beloved son. Relax. Why would you worry about what I would say to you? All I have to share this morning is that I love you very much." Tears came to my eyes, and my heart opened to God in a way it never had before. Needless to say, that experience started a journey that still continues today. Most days God has something to say, and He always begins by calling my name. Numerous blessings flow into my life because I can hear that voice daily as I write.

4. *Words of Scripture.* Not only can we quote the words of Scripture in prayer, but key passages can form the basis for extended personal prayer.

In the past decade or so it has become somewhat popular to pray over the Lord's Prayer. When I was a boy, we often incorporated the Lord's Prayer into other prayers. But praying over the Lord's Prayer is something different. You use the phrases of the Lord's Prayer as subjects for your prayer. An example would be to take the opening address, "Our Father," and verbally meditate on that phrase. For example:

"I am so glad I can call You 'Father.' I know You told us to call You 'Abba.' That makes me feel as if I can really share with You. It also makes me think of all those around me who haven't really had good earthly moms or dads. How can I live today in a way that lets people know how wonderful it is to think of You as 'Daddy' or 'Mommy'? You told us to call You 'Our Father.' That way I know it isn't just me that can do this, but that I have brothers and sisters too . . ."

So it goes on—for as long as you feel moved to pray.

You can do the same with any passage of Scripture, but familiar ones such as the twenty-third psalm are particularly meaningful. Not only does this deepen our appreciation of Scripture—praying it in ways like this drives the message home to our hearts in a new way and gives us fresh insights into the deep meaning of the text.

5. *Simple Prayers.* Prayers don't have to be long and/or elaborate to be powerful instruments of communion. Neither do they need to be always newly worded or said only once. Traditional or tried and true prayers can be valuable ways of communion as can be prayers that we say again and again.

While it is true that Jesus did state in Matthew 6:7 that Christians should not use "vain repetitions" (KJV) in their praying, the emphasis is on vain or meaningless, not on the word repetition. A more accurate translation would be the RSV: "Do not heap up empty phrases." The idea here is that we should not believe that more words or mere repetitions will make it more likely that God will hear our prayers. The short prayers I suggest here are not meaningless or empty, and any repetition suggested seeks not to force God to answer, but to deepen communion. Evidently Jesus Himself practiced repetition in His praying (Matt. 26:44).

A good example of a short prayer is the Jesus prayer. Popular in the Russian Orthodox tradition, it has spread widely in Christendom through the book *The Way of a Pilgrim.*[3] The prayer is biblically based (see Luke 18:38) and says simply: "Lord Jesus Christ, Son of God, have mercy on me, a sinner." You can shorten it even more in various ways, such as "Jesus, have mercy on me" or "Have mercy on me." The Orthodox tradition repeats the prayer, either out loud or in the heart, many, many times until eventually it moves from the head to be the constant melody of the heart, influencing all areas of life.

Francis of Assisi reputedly prayed all night saying just "Jesus, my Jesus."

Another method of simple praying is the use of one's own breathing, a form often called the breath prayer. Since most religious traditions practice it, can we consider it Christian? Yes, if the content and context are Christian. The way I use the prayer for myself is to pray for the infilling of the Holy Spirit. I simply say as I inhale, "Spirit of the living God" and as I exhale, "Fall afresh on me!" I find the combination of the words with my breath very powerful, especially as I remember that "spirit" means "wind" or "breath." We can employ any scriptural words. In fact, we pray a shortened Jesus prayer. Simply inhale to "Lord, Jesus Christ" and exhale to "have mercy on me (a sinner)." I have found this type of prayer to be particularly helpful to those who are sick or in pain and for whom thinking is a burden. Inhale Jesus' peace or love and exhale fear or pain, etc. The simple concentration on breathing and the reception of love and the expelling of pain makes a real difference to people and brings a sense of God's presence.

6. The Body at Prayer. Wholism is a biblical concept. We are whole people, and the body is part of all life, including the spiritual. The body itself can pray or at least be a complementary part of prayer.

Any kind of repetitious activity can be an occasion for prayer. Many people pray as they walk. For some time I prayed as I jogged around a track. (Of course, we would not want to do it on a street with dangerous traffic!) On one occasion I followed a teacher of Buddhism around campus and could see him meditate and pray during his measured pacing, and wondered why Christians don't do it more often.

Just as we discovered earlier in our discussion of worship, we have seen that body motion can contribute to the experience. Why not change body position in prayer to fit what is going on—prostration or bowing down during repentance, a lifting of hands during praise, open hands to receive as we make petition, etc.? All such acts bring more of us into what we are doing.

One simple, often forgotten, way that we can use our body in prayer is to pray out loud. Using the voice to actually speak our prayers would for many be very helpful. The least it could do might be to help overcome sleepiness during prayer time. I think one of the reasons Jesus sought a solitary place to pray is that He did most of His praying out loud. He did not want to awaken the entire household by His morning prayers. We may face similar challenges, but to find a place where we can speak privately to God out loud would positively influence our prayer life.

7. *Art, Music, and Visual Media.* Artistically inclined people can pray through art. I have a friend who finds communion with God as he sketches and draws images related to nature and God. Creating a work of art as an act of devotion is very real for some, whether it be a painting, a sculpture, or a piece of music. Such things do fit the definition of prayer given earlier as a reaching out to touch God. After all, we accept songs as prayers, so why not widen that to include these other kinds of devotion as well?

For those of us who may not be so good at creating art, meditation on art or some visual piece can perform much the same function. At a recent seminar a group of us spent time quietly contemplating a painting of the biblical story of the rich young ruler. We had a deeply fulfilling experience.

I have hanging in my office at home the cross-shaped weathered root of a pine tree that I found during a meaningful spiritual retreat. I find contemplation of the cross of Christ made real as I look at that piece of wood that tangibly reminds me both of my past experience and of what Jesus did at Golgatha.

None of these types of prayer are required or necessary for Christian growth or authentic Christian prayer. I offer them only as ways to commune with God that, if they are Spirit-led, can enhance greatly the interchange we have with Him, just as learning about new ways to communicate with other humans may enhance those relationships. Years of teaching spiritual formation have taught me that finding new ways to meet God often gives exciting new dimensions to the spiritual life, bringing both joy and authentic freshness.

---

[1] Herbert Lockyer, *All the Prayers of the Bible* (Grand Rapids: Zondervan, 1959), p. 5.

[2] See God compared to a mother hen in Matthew 23:37 and Luke 13:34.

[3] *The Way of a Pilgrim: and the Pilgrim Continues His Way*, trans. Helen Bacovcin (New York: Image Books, 1978).

Chapter 5

Prayer and Meditation II

"Without meditation I only think about the situation I am praying about. Meditation puts me in a different room altogether."

"I have received a profound revelation: prayer is a 'gift from God.'"

—Fellow Spiritual Pilgrims

Many Christians misunderstand, neglect, and even fear meditation. I do not understand all the reasons for such reactions, but the word has acquired a questionable if not negative connotation for large numbers of believers in Christ. Unfortunately, many such individuals lose a vital path of connection with God and accept a narrowed view of prayer. Satan is overjoyed if people become enamored over false ways of meditation, but he rejoices just as much if people reject the concept altogether. The result of both wrong paths is tragic. Christianity, especially its Protestant stream, needs a renewal of true meditation to revitalize its spiritual life and practice. A major step toward recovery of the vital practice is to realize that the Bible not only discusses and teaches meditation, but also calls—yes, even commands—us to meditate.

The Old Testament and Meditation

More than 15 times the classic King James Version translates forms of the two Hebrew words *chagah* and *siyach* as "meditate."[1] Interestingly enough, *chagah* occurs more than 30 times in the KJV. The most widely known passage containing *chagah* is God's command to Joshua to "meditate on it [the Book of the Law] day and night so that you may be careful to do everything written in it" (Joshua 1:8).

What amazes many people is to find that *chagah* literally means to "mutter, moan, or ponder (by talking to yourself) or reading in an undertone."[2] We meditate on God's Word by quietly repeating or mulling it over and over, as one would a catchy tune. In this way it has a continual influence and presence in our consciousness and life.

The other Hebrew word, *siyach*, comes closer to our common understanding of meditation with its meaning of "to be concerned with" or "occupation with one's thoughts" or "attention with something."[3]

Another Hebrew word never translated into English as "meditate" but that in some contexts clearly implies a form of meditative practice is *zakar* ("to remember").

"In some contexts *I remember* refers to the prayerful activity before God of recalling what he has revealed to and done for Israel, with the aim of considering the implications for the present (e.g., Ps. 63:6; 137:6)."[4]

Scripture considers such practices not only as special Sabbath activities (Deut. 5:15) but as something done on a daily basis (Deut. 11:18-21).

These words tell us several things about meditation in the Old Testament. *First, the biblical definition of meditate is a broad one.* It encompasses quiet or silent thought as well as verbal expression of God's Word during the activities of everyday life. As a result, it seems that the Bible regards a wide variety of things as forms of meditation.

Second, God definitely calls His people to practice meditation, as we clearly see in Old Testament times. It is not simply a Christian practice. Jewish writer Aryeh Kaplan claims in his book *Jewish Meditation* that there exists ample evidence that meditation practices were "widespread" among Jews from the biblical to the premodern era. He claims further that in the biblical world a large proportion of Israelites participated in such practices.[5]

Third, the primary subjects of meditation were God's acts, law, and/or Word. The main biblical book for meditation was clearly the Psalms. A combination of prayer, music, and meditation based on the Psalter furnished Israelites with a rich variety of ways to experience an ongoing sense of God's presence.

The New Testament and Meditation

Although the New Testament has no specific word usually translated into English as "meditate," we have evidence to support its practice by early Christians.

The most basic reason is simply that Jesus, His 12 apostles, and Paul were all Jews, steeped in the beliefs, traditions, and practices of their people. Realizing that the classic portrayal of a Jewish religious life included meditation on God and His teaching made it an expected practice. For them "prayer" in its fullest sense included what we would call both prayer and meditation. Beyond that, careful examination of the New Testament evidence implies that believers practiced meditation.

One example is the Gospel account of the preparatory experience in Jesus' life that we often label the three temptations (see Matt. 4:1-11; Mark 1:12, 13; Luke 4:1-13). The passages specifically mention only one spiritual practice, and that is "fasting" (Matt. 4:2; Luke 4:2). Fasting most often accompanied prayer and meditation (see, for example, Matt. 17:21). The whole story makes it clear that what is at issue is the nature of Jesus' identity and call. In this pivotal incident at the outset of His ministry He must know clearly who He is, what He is to do, and how He is to do it. Jesus finds His answer to all three questions in God's Word—Hebrew Scripture. Jesus had no scrolls with Him, yet all of His answers to Satan came from Scripture and were prefaced by "It is written." What seems clear is that, like many Jews of His day, Jesus had memorized much Scripture, and in those 40 days of test, trial, and crucial consideration of His ministry, He meditated deeply and profoundly on Scripture. The result was a biblical response to Satan's temptation, which itself included a false scriptural interpretation. In other words, Jesus' prolonged and intense meditation on Scripture produced not only a deep understanding of its meaning but also a personal appropriation of its teaching, which applied its truth to His life and ministry. It is a clear example of what true meditation can do for believers who follow the same practice.

Not only did Jesus practice meditation—He called for in His teachings such actions that, if followed, would include the practice of meditation.

Jesus summoned people to do at least five specific things that, if heeded, would actually either directly involve the process of meditation or produce its work in one's life.[6]

First, Jesus called people to "consider." "Look at the birds of the air" (Matt. 6:26), He declares, and "consider the lilies of the field" (verse 28,

KJV). Jesus then draws lessons that deal with life and faith. Such insights can come only from thoughtful meditation or contemplation, something that has gone beyond just a casual notice of nature.

Second, Jesus often called His audience to "hear." He clearly speaks at the end of the Sermon on the Mount of everyone who, He says, "*hears* these words of mine and does them" (Matt. 7:24, RSV). Such people Jesus describes as "wise." Hearing obviously means more than just listening or even just cognitive understanding. To hear means to have thought over, digested, and applied His words to one's life. In other words, *to have meditated* [having "heard" means having meditated] on the words to the point that one now practices and follows them.

Third, Jesus called people to "obey." Time and again in the Gospels He gives commands to others, especially to His disciples. Obedience can be an automatic conditioned response that comes with little or no thought. But the obedience that Jesus spoke about is different. When Jesus commanded/called people such as Simon and Andrew to "follow me" (see Mark 1:17), we must assume that it included prior knowledge and thought. Jesus had already been preaching and had become known. The potential disciples had already considered various issues involving Him. They had pondered and meditated many things. Any time an adult faces a radical life change, we must expect that it has been contemplated and meditated on.

Fourth, Jesus called people to see and understand. He told many parables in His ministry, including them to give insight into the nature and purpose of His ministry and the kingdom of God. By their very nature of not being direct teaching, parables demanded meditation to truly discover their implications. Discerning the "secret of the kingdom of God" (Mark 4:11) that the parables revealed required careful thought and extensive insight. The lack of understanding of the disciples at the end of Jesus' ministry shows that they had not done the required meditation on His parables and teaching, and that their "seeing" and "understanding" was still faulty.

Fifth, Jesus called people to remember. Both Old and New Testaments testify to the importance of remembering the major festivals of Israel, which memorialized God's mighty acts on the nation's behalf. Thus it is only natural that when Jesus instituted the Lord's Supper, His command was "do this in remembrance of me" (Luke 22:19). Participation in the meal would trigger a memory of the event and a pondering of its significance as well as a renewal of its meaning—all responses part and parcel of meditation. Reliving and reexperiencing the presence and life of Jesus through meditation and ritual act revitalize our religious life and prepare us to serve.

In summary, what we can say is that Jesus did not propose any specific type of meditation. I think He assumed that His hearers had already known and practiced such methods in their Jewish context.

What He did instead was teach, preach, and act in such a way that meditation became necessary to understand and follow Him and His message.

The obvious conclusion is that meditation is not only a biblical teaching but that God expects it of believers and that it becomes necessary if we are to understand and apply His Word and will at a deeper level.

What Is Meditation?

I like Peter Toon's shorthand definition of Christian meditation as "moving with the mind into the heart." Toon enlarges on the concept to say that "meditation is thus a particular way of receiving the revealed and dynamic Word of God into the heart from the mind so as to direct the will in the way of God's guidance. It is related to, but not identical with, intellectual Bible study and prayer."[7]

I would add two things to his excellent definition. First, biblical admonitions to "consider the lilies" and other parables from nature seem to suggest that not only is God's Word, the Bible, the subject of meditation, but also that God's created world of nature, while secondary, is a proper focus of meditation.

Second, meditation methods can be very diverse. As prayer can take place individually or in groups; so can meditation. Later in this chapter I will give an example of a way that a group can meditate on Scripture. Meditation can mean repeating silently or in an undertone a Bible text as you go through your everyday life. It can involve taking special time to sit quietly in your study or in the woods to ponder silently and deeply God's Word and/or His acts. All these and many more practices can be meditation. You can even develop or evolve your own methods.

Purpose and Benefits of Meditation

Meditation is a key part of study and application of the Word of God. The proper sequence of serious Bible study must include meditation. Many only read Scripture. I suggest that to understand it deeply, reading is only step one. Memory is step two, followed by meditation as step three. Remembering, which Scripture always depicts as something active with characteristics very close to obedience, is step four. Altogether it is a process by which we become, as the Bible says, "doers of the word, and not hearers only" (James 1:22, RSV; see also Rom. 2:13). Meditation is a key part of the process by which words read on a page or heard in a church become a molding, life-changing experience in our daily lives.

Meditation is a vital component to prayer. By showing us our needs in the light of Scripture and by giving us subjects for personal prayer, meditation can lead us into prayer. It can open the way to intercessory prayer by laying on our hearts the needs of others. As we rest in God's promises after we have sought His blessing, it consummates prayer. And finally, it allows us to relax quietly in God's presence when we have no words to say. In all these ways and more meditation goes hand in hand with prayer as a necessary partner.

Meditation is a key way of practicing the presence of God. For many, devotion is the quick reading of an inspirational book and a hasty prayer that makes their needs and desires known. But meditation slows that hasty, often superficial pace, and lets us begin really listening to God and sensing His will and His presence.

Whatever its forms, meditation slows us down and focuses our attention on spiritual things. In meditation we "tune out" distraction and "tune in" to God. We shut out things that would lead us away from a sense of God's presence and at the same time beam our consciousness into God's "channel." As a result we can wait on the Lord and enter His presence in a way not possible with hasty, superficial approaches.

Meditation gives life and health to body, mind, and heart in a stressful world. Most of us live pushed and hurried lives, and meditation slows us down. It becomes an oasis of calm, quiet, and rest in God in the midst of a hectic existence. Such a pause not only refreshes the spiritual life but is a boon to mental and physical health.

In summary, one can say that meditation is a key part in Christian devotion growth. All of the above benefits of meditation comprise elements of the overall path to Christian maturity. God does not desire us to meditate just because He has decided that we should. The practice of meditation is His gift to help us commune with Him so that we may grow in spirituality and in ability to minister to others.

Eastern and Western Meditation

With the rising popularity in North America and Europe of Eastern and New Age religions, questions about meditation have increased. Something that many Christians may earlier have simply neglected they now fear as a subtle way to bring false teaching into the church.

My response is that meditation is like music. A powerful tool for either good or evil, it can be God's means for growth and inspiration or the devil's instrument of deception and destruction. Let us look then at the distinctions between Eastern/New Age meditation and true Christian meditation.

The differences stem from contrasting concepts of God. Eastern religions are monistic, a form of pantheism. It means that God is present in everything and is an impersonal cosmic consciousness rather than a personal being, as in the Christian concept. Eastern meditation attempts to get in touch with and nurture this divine consciousness inside of oneself. What is sought in most cases is pure awareness without thought, the emptying of self, and the experience of mystic consciousness deep within.

On the other hand, Christian meditation seeks communion with a personal God who enters and fills us at our invitation. It begins with thoughts about His presence, Word, and works, but does not end there. While Eastern meditation searches for the "true" self, Christian meditation seeks the true God's infilling and the transformation that His presence brings.

At times we will notice occasional similarities between Eastern and Western meditation. Some postures or actions can benefit both types. Certainly the commitment to meditation by many Eastern religion devotees could serve as an inspiration to Christians. Similar health benefits can result from both streams. In the end, however, the philosophical basis, subject of meditation, and the final aim of the practice will remain different and must never be overlooked. My greatest fear is that suspicion of false meditation may lead sincere Christians to neglect the true forms of this wonderful practice and miss out on its blessings. What more powerful way to reach out to the practitioners of Eastern meditation than inviting them to experience true Christian meditation.

Eastern Meditation	**Western/Christian Meditation**
Presupposes impersonal pantheistic Cosmic Consciousness	Presupposes personal God
Aims to escape thought	Begins with thought
Desires to find self and Cosmic Consciousness inside	Wants to meet God in personal relationship
No Bible	Bible central

The "How to" of Meditation

Multitudes of potential methods for meditation exist, but I want to outline two major possibilities to give an example of what you can do. You can modify both of them to fit your particular need and preference.

The first is a variation of an ancient Christian method called *lectio divina,* or sacred/divine reading. One reason I use it is that either an individual or a group can employ it. Often I find people are more willing to try meditation personally if they have had a good experience in a group setting. In class I have often done this type as a means of introducing meditation and of helping people see the discipline's value. I make the following suggestions in the context of a group, but will include notes on how an individual can adapt it.

Pick an appropriate Bible passage. Particularly at the beginning, as an introduction to meditation, the passage should be short. That means a phrase or partial verse is fine, and initially I would not go longer than one verse. Simple, familiar passages are "I am the light of the world" (John 8:12), "God so loved the world, that he gave his only begotten Son" (John 3:16, KJV), or "The Lord is my shepherd; I shall not want" (Ps. 23:1).

Pay attention to place and posture. It is best to have a location with minimal interruptions. We may need to close doors or windows and deal with noise factors. During periods of silence any interruption will seem greatly amplified. If we do meditation in a class, latecomers must know that they'll need to wait outside until the meditation has concluded. Those participating in the meditation must assume a comfortable position that decreases their need to move or shift position. For most, that is sitting upright with back straight and both feet flat on the floor, hands comfortably placed on lap or thighs.

Begin with brief prayer for God's presence, guidance, and protection from any evil influence. When we become quiet and open to God, we simply want to make sure that anything that happens is under Jesus' leadership. The prayer itself helps to quiet people and create the setting for meaningful meditation.

Help people begin to focus on the present situation in preparation to hear God's Word. Sometimes called "centering down," it seeks to minimize distraction and let people concentrate as much as they can on God's Word. For example, suggest that they close their eyes. Also I ask people to relax their bodies consciously and to give any physical tension over to Jesus. Often shoulders and neck in particular need to release their tautness. Occasionally people should take a few deep slow breaths or become conscious of their breathing. I remind them that we have invited Jesus' presence and that He delights to be where invited and His Word cherished. I urge them to savor that presence.

Repeatedly read, meditate on, and respond to God's Word. I state—especially if it is a first-time experience for them—that the Scripture passage will be presented three times. Then I preface each reading by saying "Hear the word of the Lord" and then repeating the passage slowly and with expression. Each reading has a period of silence afterward. Finally, I will ask a question, and whoever feels moved can respond with a word or phrase—but not more than a sentence. Brevity, especially with a large group, must be emphasized. When the responses cease or slow down, the second reading takes place, and the same sequence of silence, question, and short responses follows. The third reading proceeds similarly.

The three questions I ask follow a sequence or progression, but you can modify them as needed. The first question is simply: "What is God saying in this passage?" It encourages meditation on the context of the passage. The second question begins personal application and asks: "How does this verse touch your life?" The third question not only implies personal application but invites active response to God's Word: "What command or invitation for personal action do you find in this verse?" I have found that the responses to these questions can be amazing as the Spirit works to apply Scripture to the heart and life.

Individuals can employ much the same procedure. They can read the passage themselves or record and play it, then speak aloud or jot down their responses in a journal for future reference. The ability to forget one's surroundings is easier in a group, since one does not need to think about reading, writing, or remembering the questions. But with practice you can easily learn personal *lectio.*

In conclusion, thank God in prayer for His Word and His guidance. This is a nice way to climax the experience and bring a sense of closure. Afterward people can open their eyes and move around.

If it seems appropriate, the group can share and discuss the experience they have just had. This allows time for questions and discussions of the experience's benefits and challenges. I have found that repetition of it yields increasing benefits.

One of my most memorable experiences I have had using this method occurred during the daily devotional period for a group of 14 students in a two-week Doctor of Ministry seminar. For 10 days we meditated together on God's call to Jeremiah in Jeremiah 1:4-19. The passage was especially appropriate for ministers, because they need constant renewal of their divine call. At the end of the period student after student said that Jeremiah 1 would never be the same for them again. Their call and the words of the biblical prophet had come alive and been renewed as together we meditated deeply on the prophet's words.

The second method of meditation uses visualization. While some may misunderstand or misuse visualization and imagination, both approaches can also be powerful meditation tools. Negatively, visualization can be used to control or manipulate other people, but employed positively, it can bring life to God's Word and nature. Imagination can either lead to worthless daydreaming or help us to appreciate and understand Bible stories more fully.

The same guidelines that apply to *lectio divina* apply to visualization. Visualization should be connected to Scripture or nature. It is simply common sense that when Christ tells us to "consider the lilies" we must either have actual plants in hand or picture our past experience with them. If we want to remember the acts of God, how can we do so without visualizing them? Or if we meditate on the passion of Christ, can we do so without a mental image of the event? Properly used, a sanctified imagination and visualization guided by Scripture is a tremendous asset to the spiritual life.

This method is particularly helpful in connection with the biblical stories. I have found time and time again in my own experience that study and spiritual life are enriched, as I have in imagination entered the scriptural account and relived the event. Also I have seen lives changed for the better through a correct use of the method.

One of my most memorable experiences was to ask a class to spend an hour meditating on Jesus' birth story in Luke 2. All they were allowed to use was the Bible. They could reread the narrative as often as they wanted, but for the bulk of the length of time they were to meditate on the story. I urged them to picture, hear, smell, etc., as they relived the story. As final instruction, I asked them to enter the story personally and decide what they would do if they had been there.

The next day one woman in the class shared her story. Married but childless, she explained how in the end it had dawned on her that what she really wanted to do was hold the baby. Then of course, it struck her that she was cradling the Savior of the World. She testified powerfully about how a narrative that she had listened to many times since childhood had become powerful and alive in a new way. The story and the Jesus of the story had moved and changed her.

In conclusion, I appeal to you to leave aside whatever may have caused you to neglect this powerful God-given means of communion with God and deep study of His Word. Give it a try, and allow Him to use it to speak to you. Don't attempt it just once, but spend a month with it and perhaps explore it as a group. Study it further and adapt the methods that work for you, and you will find your spiritual life blessed.

---

[1] Robert Young, *Analytical Concordance to the Bible* (New York: Funk and Wagnalls Co.), pp. 651, 652.

[2] William L. Holladay, ed., *A Concise Hebrew and Aramaic Lexicon of the Old Testament* (Grand Rapids: Eerdmans, 1971), p. 76.

[3] *Ibid.*, pp. 350, 351.

[4] Peter Toon, *From Mind to Heart: Christian Meditation Today* (Grand Rapids: Baker, 1987), p. 24.

[5] Aryeh Kaplan, *Jewish Meditation: A Practical Guide* (New York: Schocken Books, 1985), pp. 40-42.

[6] Compare items 1, 2, 4, and 5 with Toon, pp. 47, 48.

[7] Toon, p. 10.

Chapter 6

Study and Guidance

"At the spiritual retreat, as I sat down and reflected on my past, I could hardly see to write because of the tears in my eyes. I cried a little because I was able to see hands of God active in my life."

"God has a way of reviving our spirit and mending our broken souls if we allow Him to."

—Fellow Spiritual Pilgrims

Introduction

Meditation is one way to hear God's word and voice. It is appropriate to follow a chapter on meditation with one on guidance because they go together. Study and listening to God's guidance in other ways than meditation are crucial parts of communication, which lies at the heart of the spiritual life.

While study may not immediately grab one's interest or concern, most Christians care deeply about God's guidance. The two are actually closely tied together. I find that, in general, college and university students faced with many decisions often wonder what God's will for them is. Andrews University conducted a poll of its students while I served as a professor there. The number one religious question the students had was "How do I find God's will for my life?" A recent Christian bestseller has been Henry Blackaby and Claude King's *Experiencing God.*[1] The subtitle gives a more accurate picture of the volume's content: *How to Live the Full Adventure of Knowing and Doing the Will of God.* In other words, the book is about guidance—finding the divine will for your life.

I suggest that the discipline of study—especially Bible study—is closely connected with that. We read the Bible and devotional literature so that we may know what God desires for each of us. Let us look at these topics by first of all considering the discipline of study and then becoming more focused by asking how one builds on that study and other means to determine God's will for our lives.

True Study

Most, especially those who are presently going to school, would agree that much of what passes for "study" is highly superficial. A hasty cramming of the short-term memory with a list of facts does little to fix major concepts in mind or to change one's life. In fact, school often militates against true study, as seen from the standpoint of spiritual discipline.

True study, which involves the spiritual art of listening to God, is quite different from the scholarly examination of a text. Theologians and students of religion often delve into what they call exegesis (from the Greek, meaning to "guide out" of the text). Exegesis is the careful process of discerning the meaning of the text by examining the words, content, and historical background. While exegesis can be *part* of true study, it is not the whole. The complete study must include personal involvement, application, and action as we apply original meaning to our life today. Transformation by living God's will is the goal of scriptural study.

Study also entails more than the perusal of books or texts or talk (i.e., verbal study). In a spiritual sense, study also includes the nonverbal—actions, processes, and events—in the world around us. Even more important, it involves a close analysis of our own lives and actions. God-knowledge and self-knowledge go hand in hand. Thus worthwhile study means carefully analyzing all of these things in an attempt to hear God's voice, discern His will, and apply what we have learned to our personal life. Such study is rare in our world today and would revolutionize our lives and society if it happened on a broad scale. Some do the analytical, reflective, logical part of the study and stop there. Others hastily apply Bible words without having done careful, thoughtful analysis of them. Such action may not reflect the truth and the will of God, but be based on half-truths and partial solutions.

Richard Foster[2] suggests that true study involves four steps. First comes *repetition*. No one can truly study something without going over it again and again. A good teacher always repeats anything that is crucial. People performed the key rituals of Old Testament religion again and again to fix them in the mind and to deepen reflection on them. The Lord's Supper takes place frequently because it must be thoroughly contemplated. It is more profitable to read a good book twice and make it a real part of life than to read two good books once and remember little from either.

Second, we need *concentration and attention with focused listening*. Study cannot take place with the mind in neutral or involved in simultaneous multitasking. TV watching and study do not happen together. The more focused the mind, the more profitable the study.

Third, *comprehension* is important. When we do not understand something, we must not skip it, but seek to grasp it. Things that are initially mysterious but after in-depth study become clearer are often the most meaningful part of study. We should welcome mysteries as aids to growth rather than bothersome obstacles.

Fourth, *reflection and reliving* are crucial. Such things require time and commitment. Reflection moves us beyond impulse and hurry to places where real listening can occur. Reliving and applying will move us beyond mere understanding to practical application. Only then will study really bear wonderful fruit in the life.

I would add a fifth step, which actually should be the first one. We must have a *holy purpose* in place for study to be truly study in a spiritual sense. Intellectual curiosity has nothing inherently wrong with it. A desire for facts is not evil. But study as a spiritual discipline must move far beyond mere curiosity and intellectual knowledge. The more we have fixed in our minds a desire to know God and His will for our lives, the more spiritually productive our study becomes. I have seen it happen many times. A young person begins to look at the Bible, perhaps for a class or just out of curiosity. The individual studies the content as one does a textbook in a class that holds little interest. The Bible is just another book. Then something happens—the student makes a spiritual commitment—and he or she goes back to the Bible as if the book had changed completely. Words leap off the page and burn into the heart. A bond between the text and the heart and mind takes place. The person feels drawn to plead with the Spirit for understanding, and a reborn spiritual life then commences. This is the stuff of spiritual revolution.

In conclusion, many of us read too much and study too little. I find myself led less and less to a multitude of new books, and more and more to restudy the ones that have been pivotal in my life. Whatever you find yourself doing, study of a spiritual kind should be a part of what it means to hear Jesus and to follow Him. It also is a key element in God's guidance.

Discerning God's Will/Guidance

When talking with Christians about how God guides us, I often find people at one or the other of two extremes. On the one side are those who have trouble with the belief and practice of divine guidance. While they may believe in God's general guidance or will, they have not experienced His leading in a more specific experiential way.

At the other extreme are those who glibly speak of God's will and seem to have very specific knowledge of what He wants in minute detail. God tells them regularly what to wear and where to park. These people turn off or scare those at the other extreme. We want to seek a middle way. I firmly believe that God leads—at times in great detail—but that His will is sometimes not known quickly or easily but involves careful communication and a confirmation through time of that leading in a variety of ways.

A number of barriers hinder us when it comes to discerning God's will. Knowing what they are can help us begin to remove them as we enter the discernment process.

Haste and impatience hamper guidance. In an age in which everything is instant, people want to experience God's guidance *now.* They may talk to Him, but they find little or no time to listen. Silence, solitude, and a reflective, open spirit are not part of their prayers. They are like the person who knocks at the door but runs away before the homeowner can get to it.

Unbelief is a barrier to guidance. If you don't believe that God is active in human life, it makes no sense to seek His guidance. Some, while holding nominal Christian beliefs, have, down deep, accepted a secular worldview that denies any divine activity. If you don't believe in God's guidance, you won't seek it. And you can be sure that you won't recognize it unless He hits you with an obvious heavenly vision.

Ignorance is a barrier to guidance. As with other spiritual disciplines, some have received no detailed instruction about how God leads. Lacking knowledge or clear teaching, they are at a loss about how to seek God's voice. This chapter seeks to help solve this problem.

Fear can lead many away from God's guidance. People are afraid of various things. Some worry that they may be deceived and not really find out God's will. Others fear that what God asks of them may be weird or embarrassing. Many are not sure they'll be willing to follow His will, so it's easier not to know it. Still others dread what their life might be like if they truly follow God and His will. Several of these fears may infect a person's thinking and cause a barrier to truly seeking God's guidance.

Selective listening can be a problem. It is possible to seek God's will only about pleasant things. He, on the other hand, may choose to reveal to us our needs or our sins. Some don't want to hear this part of His voice. For God to speak to us fully, we must be prepared to hear all that He has to say.

Unwillingness to test supposed guidance can be a barrier. The Bible gives us certain ways to determine whether what we think is God's voice is truly from Him. When we go with our first, quick impression and don't take time to experience things truly, we will make mistakes. Such problems bring disillusionment and cause us to shrink from seeking Him and His way for our lives.

Those who honestly seek God's will move beyond such barriers to develop an ear that will listen carefully and deliberately. They are open to God and expect and desire Him to speak. I believe that He will not disappoint them, but will respond when they call. He will answer in one or more ways. Individuals who do seek God's will and follow it will find a peace and fulfillment that can come in no other way.

Ways That God Guides

Some of the myriad ways that God speaks follow. He may use only one method, but often I find that He employs a combination of them to get through to us.

God speaks through the Bible. The Bible not only gives us the general picture of His will for us, but He uses it in other ways. When we preface

Bible study with prayer and an honest attempt to follow God's will, the Holy Spirit can bring things to our heart and mind that we have never seen before. Most of us have had the experience of going back over a Bible story or passage that we have read or heard previously but suddenly, maybe even unexpectedly, something in the passage strikes our heart with a strange power. Insight that we did not have before comes to us, and we are blessed and led as the Spirit drives home God's word to the heart. Perhaps reading the Bible on our knees as George Whitefield did may help this happen more often. Bible study is not merely about facts and information, but is hearing God's voice and changing our life.

Silence, solitude, and quiet create space for God to speak. Our contention in this book has been that prayer or any communication with God must be two-way. Listening as well as speaking is particularly important in the process of finding divine guidance. To listen truly, we must be silent, and as many other voices as possible must be silenced as well. That is what solitude is about and why Jesus often sought it (see, for example, Mark 1:35; 6:46). Lonely hills and other spots distanced Christ from the clamoring voices of both the needy and His enemies and allowed Him to focus more easily on God's still small voice. All would receive great benefit from having a readily available space away from the noise of life—even if it is only a closet. Times there can refresh us as nothing else.

A continual presence of God's voice within can guide us. We are not talking about a passing impression but rather a special, persistent inner push. While hard to define, it is the sudden sense that God is strongly nudging you, and it arises deep inside rather than off the top of your head. I find this has happened most often to me in my encounters with people. Either I have felt led to talk with someone I wasn't planning to, or something has pushed me to say something in conversation that I had not planned but that turned out to be particularly appropriate. At other times I have been in a bookstore or library, and a particular book or journal has seemed to jump out at me and I know something there has a message for me. To guard against error and mere natural impressions, we need to test such "risings" by the criteria that we will soon discuss.

Journaling can be a key factor in guidance. Chronicling our inner journey, journaling does not merely record daily events like a diary (although that can be part of it) but talks about the meaning behind and significance of them. Some people greatly benefit from journaling and take to it naturally. For others it takes effort and time, but eventually it becomes a powerful spiritual factor. I fit into the latter category. Initially I felt silly recording daily events until suddenly I broke through beyond the events to start writing my deeper inner journey.

Such journaling can help us know God's will and sense His guidance in several ways.

One is by enabling us to remember and to reflect on what He has done. The act of reflecting on the day and seeing when God was in it can trigger insight into divine action and guidance.

I follow a very simple practice in seeking God's guidance daily with my journal as a tool. After writing whatever seems important, I stop and say, "Lord, do You have anything You want to say to me?" To this day, I find the practice to be a powerful one in my life, and I look forward to hearing regularly what God speaks. Sometimes there is very little. Often the message is general—"live in My love," for example. At times it can be specific: "Jon, you have not been thoughtful to Kathy, your wife, recently." If it is an important message, one that may be challenging to follow, I may hear it again and again. During my recent bout with cancer I have come to realize how impatient I am and how I push myself and, often, others. Repeatedly in my journal God has said "Relax" or "Slow down" or "Rest in Me," and has shown me how my constant pushing is a lack of faith in His guidance, timing, and ability to bring things to pass.

God speaks to us through visions and dreams. We find numerous examples of this in Scripture, and it is not limited to the lives of prophets and apostles. Joseph, husband of Mary, had more than one dream of guidance (Matt. 1:20; 2:13, 19). Joel 2:28 looks to a time when "your old men will dream dreams" and "your young men will see visions." Peter, in his Pentecost sermon (Acts 2:16, 17), announces that the Joel message is being fulfilled now. The implication is that large numbers of people will receive guidance this way.

Because of history and culture, many in the West avoid or ignore this means of guidance. It is questionable, they say, and open to counterfeit and misuse. Interestingly enough, most non-Western cultures—especially Africa and Asia—highly regard and regularly practice this form of divine leading. I find that international students in my classes respond enthusiastically to a discussion of visions and dreams and can readily cite instances during which God has lead in this way.

Interestingly, God has used this method to speak to people who may not be followers of Jesus. I talked at length to a missionary who spent years in a North African Islamic country. Officially he served as pastor to the expatriate European community, but in his heart he hoped to share Jesus with local Muslims. The government prohibited overt evangelism, so he simply prayed for God to send him those who needed to hear the message. Soon people began to approach him—some talked to him as he did business in town, while others came to his home or the church. Most of them did so at the prompting of visions or dreams. They would see the missionary in a dream, and a voice would tell them to talk to him. Others would have a vision of the church sign and receive a command to go and seek truth there. By various dreams and visions, mostly to university students, God sent more than 20 people in the first year. The least that can be said is that we should be open to God's use of this means to speak His Word to us.

Nature can speak to us of God's will. While in most cases this avenue of God's revelation to us is more general in scope, we still need to be alert and aware of it. At times it can serve the purpose of preparing us to hear Him in other ways. Most of us have sensed the power of God in awesome mountain vistas or the beauty of a forest. Jesus constantly used examples from nature to teach spiritual lessons, and it is logical to believe that He still does so. Many find it particularly helpful, during a time of crisis or of crucial decisions, to go to a place of natural beauty and there seek God.

Engaging in ministry can reveal God's will to us. I have seen many young people find their God-given vocation by spending some time in ministry. If you think you might like to teach for God, try it. Or if you are interested in nursing and not sure about it, find a way to work in a place in which healing ministry occurs.

For those who are already serving, God at times reveals His way and speaks as we open ourselves to His voice in the process of ministry. I find that sometimes as I write sermons it becomes obvious that God is leading with words, and speaks even as I am engaged in the very act of composing them. Time and again while counseling with people, I find words and ideas emerging that are really not mine but that come from the Spirit. In the process of ministry itself, God reveals His will and guides us.

Providential events are ways that God guides. A missed airplane, a chance meeting, or an unexpected development can all turn out to be God's appointments. It has taken me a while to learn this, but such unplanned events do not distress me as they once did. I have learned by experience that God often uses such things to lead us in directions that we may not have even dreamed of before.

Praying and fasting are key elements in God's guidance. Since we have already discussed these disciplines in detail, we do not need to say much, except to remind ourselves that one of the functions of prayer and meditation is to listen to God so that we may discern His guidance and have the courage to follow it.

God's guidance can come to us through other people of faith. This can happen through a single person, such as a sensitive spouse or a wise spiritual guide. Or it can occur through a number of people, such as a small group at our church that knows us. As we look at the decision or challenge we face and wonder what God would have us do, we can usually profit by sharing our need with others and seeking their guidance.

Richard Foster's book on the spiritual disciplines lists guidance as one of the corporate disciplines.[3] He believes that we have taught often on the subject of individual guidance but need special help on the frequently neglected corporate guidance.

Foster certainly has a biblical basis for promoting corporate guidance. Matthew 18:19, 20 clearly shows that it makes a difference when believers agree on spiritual issues. The call for Paul and Barnabas to serve as missionaries comes in a corporate context as fellow believers pray, fast, and worship together (Acts 13:1-3). Acts 15 gives a corporate model for seeking God's guidance in major issues that the church must confront.

Quakers have what some term "meetings for clearness," in which individuals with a question can seek help from fellow believers. After a sharing of the problem, the group prays, worships, and discusses their thoughts with the questioner. Even if a clear decision does not emerge, the seeker has a built-in support group to continue to pray and assist him or her as he or she seeks God's will.

Clear recognition of divine guidance through groups can cast church committees and board meetings in a new light. What if everyone there saw their time together as a corporate occasion of seeking God's guidance rather than a chance to advocate their ideas and plans for the church? It would undoubtedly lead to more prayer, worship, and humility as the meeting became a place to hear God speak.

Most of us would find much benefit if we made more use of the corporate guidance model in our lives.

Testing God's Guidance

When we become convinced that God does, in fact, communicate with us and guide our lives, there needs to be a corresponding interest in knowing how to test such divine leading. How can we know for sure that it truly comes from God and not our own desires or, worse yet, is something demonic? Such a process is not an exact science, but it does seem that there do exist both biblical and rational principles that can help us as we try to sort out the issues.

New guidance, if it's true, will not contradict past divine leading. The primary example of this is the Bible. For Christians who accept it as an authority it serves as a check on new revelation. Thus, for example, the man who claims that God has told me to divorce my wife and marry my secretary is suggesting that he has been guided in a way contradictory to Bible teaching. Therefore I must reject his alleged new guidance.

Wise individuals with a good relationship with God are often a help in evaluating potential counsel. As mentioned above, godly people can be a source of guidance, and for the same reasons they can also serve as evaluators of other guidance. That is one of the reasons the church (the body of believers) exists—that it may offer mutual help in walking the Christian way.

Reason can also help us. A person who claims that God is telling him or her to be a gospel singer needs to have a good singing voice. Lacking such a voice, one can validly question the source of the "call." One can ask, "Does the supposed guidance fit the person's talents, abilities, and situation?" While such an approach does not rule out the possibility of God working miraculously (suddenly endowing a person with a talent he or she did not have before), it does require us to think things through.

One should consider previous events. Does this guidance fit with how God has led in our life in the past? Do we have record of receiving guidance that proves to be true? If the answer is yes to both questions, it increases the chance that the new guidance is also valid.

The mental state of key players is crucial. If people are highly stressed, overly tired, and in a challenging situation, hearing God's voice becomes more difficult. The possibility of error increases as the stress and confusion rise. In such a case, they may need some kind of delay to help them have time to really hear God when the pressure is off.

Just one final observation. In my experience, God most often begins by guiding us ourselves rather than using us to lead others. The person who first "hears God" and has a message for someone else always raises questions in my mind. Receiving messages for others is closer to what we would call prophecy and not guidance. Personal discernment of God's will and leading comes in most cases before we receive messages for other people.

Conclusion

God does want to guide your life. If you truly believe that He is love, you will want Him to do so and will do your best to facilitate it. Your fulfillment in life will be in direct proportion to your willingness to follow wherever He leads.

I have had a number of people come to me concerned that they have not heard (or perhaps even rejected) God's message to them and therefore are not and cannot be in His will. My basic message to them is that He is so eager for us to hear that He keeps on calling. God doesn't speak once and then blithely say to us, if we miss it or don't heed it, "Too bad for you—you had your chance." Notice the call of Samuel as told in 1 Samuel 3:2-10. At first Samuel thinks that he has heard only the high priest Eli. Three times the lad believes that the divine voice is a human one. He had not yet received revelation from God, so he just didn't know God's voice. Finally, following the advice of Eli, his elderly spiritual mentor, Samuel says, "Speak, for your servant is listening." God's message then comes. The point is that God speaks repeatedly and does not give up easily.

If we desire to listen to God and He has an important message, He will give it as often as needed. He wants us to hear, and may use others as well as repetition to help us recognize what is going on. With that principle in mind, we may eagerly and persistently seek His guidance, knowing that He will respond and that we can live in the center of His will.

---

[1] Henry T. Blackaby and Claude V. King, *Experiencing God* (Nashville: Broadman and Holman, 1994).

[2] Richard Foster, *Celebration of Discipline* (New York: HarperCollins, 1998).

[3] *Ibid.*, pp. 175ff.

Chapter 7

Community

"In our journey with God, we are always in the company of other believers."

"I began to experience temptation much more strongly, and I realized that one big reason was simply that I was lonely. So my wife and I began a small group . . . and I can confirm that the community was what I was missing."

"The prayers of my small group have led to some significant healing of childhood emotional damage and to my victory over tobacco!"

—FELLOW SPIRITUAL PILGRIMS

According to the first chapter of the Bible, God saw that it was not good for the first man, Adam, to be alone. So the Lord created Eve, the first woman. From the beginning, being constantly alone has not been good for anyone. While solitude is helpful at times, we must balance it with community. God's people have always had a community—a group of like believers who share and support each other. This principle especially works in the spiritual life.

In our pursuit of meeting God, we can begin to learn how actually to communicate with Him through prayer, meditation, and study. We then seek to remove any potential static in that communication through fasting, solitude, and following a life of simplicity. The next question that comes is "How can we persevere and keep growing in our life with God?" Here is where we need to think about community and the fellowship of others. While community serves many functions in the spiritual life, one of the most crucial is that it gives us the incentive and courage to grow and keep journeying in our divine quest as we meet with fellow travelers on the spiritual way. As one of my friends said, "I have begun jogging—many times. The only times I have kept jogging were the times I did it with others."

Community is not equal to the local church. While in some cases congregations do form communities or have smaller groups in their midst that experience community, many churches are social groupings that lack real fellowship. Community takes place when a group of people experience a sense of bearing each other's burdens and, as the early Methodists said, "watch over one another in love" with the aim of discipleship. For this to happen, the number of those involved must be limited. Real nurture and spiritual growth take place in groups of three to 12 or possibly a home/house church. For this reason we want to examine such small groups, especially as they relate to spiritual growth.

Biblical and Historical Basis

Jesus spent the largest portion of His time with a small band of 12 members. The choice of His group was so crucial that He spent all night in prayer before He made his final decision (Luke 6:12). According to Mark 3:13, the first thing He called them to do was to be with Him. Preaching and healing would come later, but even those grew out of close fellowship with Jesus. He knew that to leave a legacy He had to be very close to a few people, because from a practical point of view it was not possible to be intimate with a large number of them. That fellowship was what made it possible for the disciples to keep growing. At certain times He seemed to narrow His focus to a more intimate relationship with three out of those 12 (Mark 5:37).

Although the earlier Christians did at times worship in the Jewish Temple, much of their fellowship occurred in homes (Acts 2:42-44). The earliest archaeological evidence of the regular construction of church buildings comes from about A.D. 250.[1] Thus we have clear evidence that the earliest Christian worship took place among small groups in a home setting. In fact, someone has said that you cannot really understand the New Testament unless you presuppose Christians met in intimate fellowship groups in which they were personally known and loved.

It is very interesting to see the frequent efforts in churches today to revive community through small groups. Many do not realize how crucial small groups are to the growth and function of what we call megachurches. The largest local congregation in the history of Christianity—Yoido Full Gospel Church in Seoul, Korea, pastored by David Yonggi Cho—depends heavily on small home groups for discipleship and growth. So does Willow Creek Community Church, pastored by Bill Hybels and perhaps one of the most well-known North American megachurches.

Many of these groups draw inspiration from the early Methodists. John Wesley saw his "religious society" burst the borders of his native Great Britain and spread across the world. For a while Methodism was the largest denomination in North America.

Wesley did not begin with the aim of starting a new religious organization, but simply wanted to bring renewal to his beloved Anglican church. He encouraged people to attend church, but also formed them into societies made up of groups of 12 called "class meetings." The groups of 12 formed the core of the Methodist movement. In fact, Wesley refused to preach anywhere he could not enroll people in "classes."[2] In his evangelistic meetings seldom (if ever) did he ask people to make decisions for Christ. But he did invite them to join a class meeting or small group. He required only one condition to join—a desire to "'flee the wrath to come,' to know God's acceptance, and to live a higher life."[3]

People experienced two things in his class meetings. First, love and care were manifested as members looked out for both the spiritual and practical needs of others in the group. Second, they learned about accountability in their spiritual life. Each week the group leader talked about the condition of his spiritual life and openly confessed problems and failings. He then asked each class member to share their experience. The group offered prayer for all the needs of its members and gave opportunity to donate funds to help others.

The dynamism of these groups powered the rapid spread of Methodism. Many trace the decline of that zeal to the dropping of the class system and the formation of a denomination with settled, paid pastors. A number of Methodists are today trying to revive the older system with some modifications.

Meaning Today

I must admit that I was dubious when first introduced to small groups. It seemed faddish and designed for lonely people who needed companionship or therapy. But I discovered that the problem for me (and for others) was that small groups got promoted as small groups. People saw them as just another program of the church. The pastor's duty was to promote small groups and get them going. The same thing can happen for the cell church, which sees the church as needing to be organized around "cells," or small groups. One can also misunderstand the house church movement in a similar manner. The core value we are seeking is the special "loving one another" and "helping one another" kind of community that Jesus and the disciples created. Small groups, cell churches, and house churches are not the answer. Rather, community—true, intimate fellowship—is. If we see small groups and cell/house churches as forums to facilitate and preserve community, they can be part of the answer. I shrink from promoting a particular form of small groups, because community can take place through a variety of structures if people have caught its significance and are willing to use any available structure to make it happen.

The apostle Paul deliberately set up the earliest Christian communities, which often centered on house churches. For him, to embrace the gospel was to embrace community.[4] Community was not a particular program of the church—it was the reason the body came into being in the first place.

Accepting and practicing this principle would require a radical rethinking and reorganization of the Western church. To understand its implications, we can take a clearer look at the way Wesley shaped early Methodism. He had three levels of structure.[5] The largest (or top level) was the society. It comprised all the Methodists in a geographical area, town, or city. The middle level was the class, discussed earlier, consisting of not more than 12 people who met weekly. The smallest group was the "band." It could be smaller than the class and required a special commitment, usually to a particular task, such as prison ministry, etc. Historians have estimated that about 20 percent of Methodists were band members, while all were expected to be class members.

What is crucial to note is that the key to Wesley's organization was the "class"—the middle level. His call was always to join a class. Individuals could be a member of the society, join its fellowship, and partake in

Communion only if they had a card showing regular participation in the class. For Wesley, that 12-member class was the essence of church, because true community was core. For most churches today, the top-level "society," or larger church, is the core organization. If small groups exist, they are a lesser part of that church and function like the bands and special groups, involving extra commitment. When Wesley's movement became more like the surrounding culture, it too switched its emphasis to the society and lost his unique organization, which had emphasized community, honest discipleship, and love.

To recapture the life-changing, discipline-involving power of the spirit-filled early church, a renewal of community must take place. Only in such community can full spiritual development occur. That is why true community is such a vital part of our spiritual life and is the only way to long-term growth.

Putting Community Into Practice

We have already looked at some of the challenges inherent in establishing Christian community, but I believe they can be overcome. What I want to do in the concluding section of this chapter is to consider some general principles as to how we can implement community, and then examine one example from my own experience.

Catch a new vision for community and its importance to spiritual life. Go through the Gospels and/or Epistles and notice the key role of community. Look up all the New Testament passages that use the phrase "one another," one that implies community. Read about the early Methodist movement and study other churches and groups that practice Christian community. Examine the power of small groups and house churches. New practices are best spawned by a new and powerful vision of what should and can be.

Ask God to lead you to start a group that you will be a part of. You don't need to change your church or your men's/women's group. Rather, I'm suggesting that you pray that God will lead you to one to four people to whom you can approach with your vision. Actions will make your talk about community real. You need to experience it yourself.

Keep a few key principles in mind. Remember the issue is not structure but community. There are, however, some principles that should be followed. People must commit to being there. When you ask them to join, request that they try a short trial period of four to eight weeks. Many fear to make open-ended commitments to unknown things. Structure can vary, but three principles always apply: honesty/openness, love/caring, and accountability. People should never be forced to share, but if they do, it must be authentic. Care for others in the group must be evident, and—as in Wesley's group—accountability is necessary for growth. It is good to have items or goals that the group commits to. It goes without saying that whatever anyone says in the group must remain confidential.

As challenges arise, seek mentors and resources. Ask a pastor, teacher, or friend with experience to help if needed. Find books, seminars, and Internet resources that can instruct. Have a teachable attitude, be open to new ideas, but keep foremost those principles that make a difference.

For many years I regularly taught a seminary course on spirituality. From the beginning I realized the importance of community and worked through the years to find a form that would incorporate into the class structure something that would lead students to experience authentic community.

What eventually evolved and seemed to work best was launching small groups of four during a one-day retreat that took place at the beginning of the class (a doctoral dissertation describes the retreat in some detail).[6] For our purposes here, it is enough to say that outside of a short worship time of singing and breaks to eat lunch and exercise, two main activities took up most of the day. First there was quiet time for reflection and solitude. We scheduled three such periods of about one hour each. During the first hour each participant relived God's leading in their past, during the second hour they considered their current situation, and during the third we asked each what their hopes and dreams for the future were.

After spending about one hour in silence and journaling, the members met in their small groups of four to share the insights they had gained during their time of reflection. They knew that the groups would continue meeting for the duration of the quarter-long (10-week) class, so they were interested in getting to know each other. The three intense hours of small group sharing about their past, present, and future created a deep bonding. At the end, group members were embracing, exchanging phone numbers, and praying for each other. This kickoff fostered deep community for the period of the class. The groups then met weekly during the rest of the quarter. I never saw this process fail. Sometimes about halfway through the day, some began wondering what was happening, but the Holy Spirit invariably used the dynamic of really hearing and being to create bonds that not only socially nurtured but spiritually encouraged us as well.

Many of the groups continued to meet on a volunteer basis after the class ended. Lifelong friendships formed, and the participants now understood community in a deep, experiential way that could never have happened through merely theoretical means.

In our individualistic Western society, too often our spirituality has been of the Lone Ranger type. But we can more easily meet the challenges we face as we share with others and have their support. Willingness to share one another's burdens in a real way helps all Christians. Determine to begin the march from fighting spiritual challenges alone to authentic Christian community. Although the journey will have its struggles, its end will be to the glory of God as we build true fellowship.

---

[1] John Foster, *The First Advance* (London: SPCK, 1972), p. 20.

[2] George G. Hunter III, *To Spread the Power* (Nashville: Abington Press, 1988), p. 56.

[3] *Ibid.*, p. 57.

[4] Robert Banks, *Paul's Idea of Community* (Peabody, Mass.: Hendrickson Publishers, 1994), pp. 26, 27.

[5] See D. Michael Henderson, *John Wesley's Class Meeting* (Nappanee, Ind.: Francis Asbury Press, 1997), pp. 83-126.

[6] Carol M. Tasker, "The Impact of Intentional Learning Experiences for Personal Spiritual Formation on Seminary Students" (Ph.D. diss., Andrews University, 2002), pp. 155-186.

Chapter 8

Fasting

"Fasting reminds us that we are sustained by 'every word that proceeds from the mouth of God' [Matt. 4:4, RSV]."

—FELLOW SPIRITUAL PILGRIM

Fasting is not a topic that excites popular opinion—even among Christians—these days. In reality, the fasting that our society is familiar with is a far cry from the biblical concept. The neglect and misunderstanding of the topic becomes at least somewhat reasonable when we realize that there seems to have not been a single book written on Christian fasting between 1861 and 1954.[1] In this chapter I call you to consider this scriptural spiritual discipline and, perhaps, entice you to try it in your life.

Most Americans see fasting as an activity to facilitate weight loss. In Europe many fast periodically to promote health and cleansing. On the other hand, the Bible in its more than 60 references to fasting relates the practice to spiritual issues. More specifically, it is usually directly connected to prayer and often is in the context of a special need or request. This should not seem strange to us, since all major world religions, including Judaism, Islam, Hinduism, and Buddhism, utilize and promote fasting in connection with religious life.

My discussions with people have revealed that objections to fasting for spiritual reasons usually stem from two basic misunderstandings. First, many see the practice as legalism or a false attempt to manipulate God. I hear such questions as "If I fast, does that make God more likely to hear my prayers?" or "Isn't fasting just a way to make 'points' with God?" All such questions presuppose that people use it to earn God's favor or blessing, and those who raise the questions, therefore, have no interest in being a part of such a misguided endeavor.

While we must honestly admit that some may view true biblical fasting in this way and that one can abuse the practice, it is not what the Bible had in mind, as we shall shortly see.

Second, many view fasting through the lens of the extreme practice of the discipline. They read of Moses, Elijah, and Jesus fasting 40 days (Deut. 9:9; 1 Kings 19:8; and Luke 4:1, 2), and it seems both impossible to them and distant from their daily life. Perhaps they may learn of some of the abuses of the practice that arose in the Middle Ages and find themselves turned off by it. Or they may have run into a "fasting fanatic" who believes that the whole spiritual life depends on the practice.

In response, we must ask, "What are the biblical principles of fasting, and how may we apply them in our lives?"

Biblical Definition of Fasting

Fasting is, I suggest, completely, selectively, or partially refraining voluntarily from some substance (most often food and/or drink) or practice. We must notice three key issues in this definition. First, let us consider the "selectively" or "partially" refraining part. Although the prophet Daniel at other times practiced a complete fast (Dan. 9:3), during one 21-day period he ate "no delicacies" and declares, "No meat or wine entered my mouth, nor did I anoint myself at all" (Dan. 10:3, RSV). He seems to have chosen for a period to eat simple food as a partial fast during a time of spiritual crisis.

Second, fasting is not necessarily food or drink, but can be other practices as well. Notice in the previous passage that Daniel as a part of fasting does not anoint himself. Isaiah 58:6, 7, calls for people to fast by loosing the bonds of wickedness, letting the oppressed go free, sharing bread with the hungry, and bringing homeless people into their houses. Clearly, refraining from certain acts or substituting righteous acts for evil ones is a fast as well. Might not a prophet today call us to fast from television or the Internet or professional sports or soap operas or shopping?

Third, for Christians, fasting is voluntary. While the Old Testament requires corporate fasting on the Day of Atonement (see Lev. 16:29, 31) and later on other festivals (Zech. 8:19), nowhere does the New Testament command fasting. It merely points out the practice and assumes (for example, Matthew 6:16, RSV, "and when you fast") that believers will observe it as appropriate. Requiring people to fast is not a New Testament teaching.

Reasons to Fast

If Scripture does not demand it, many wonder why anyone should fast at all. I suggest a number of reasons:

Fasting is an approved biblical practice engaged in by many godly Bible characters. The more than 60 references to fasting in Scripture divide about equally between the testaments.[2]

In most cases they clearly refer to a common, valuable practice. The general Bible teaching assumes and approves the fasting of believers.

In the places that the Bible does question fasting, it does not appear to condemn the practice itself, but rather a misuse or an inappropriateness of timing. Isaiah 58 teaches that literal fasting does no good for those who live selfishly and reflect no care for the needs of the hungry and oppressed. The Sermon on the Mount (Matt. 6:16-18) challenges open fasting that publicly flaunts piety but approves fasting done only before God.

In Mark 2:18-20 Jesus teaches that at certain times ("while the bridegroom is with them" [RSV]) it is not necessary to fast. But at a later appropriate time fasting can take place. Scripture raises questions about fasting in the context of helping us understand the broader issues connected with true biblical fasting.

It may be helpful to recognize that the list of biblical personages who fasted reads like a roster of the believers' hall of fame—Moses, David, Elijah, Esther, Daniel, Anna, John the Baptist, Jesus, and Paul. Those stalwarts undoubtedly saw something valuable and helpful in the practice.

Fasting can serve as a visible sign of persistence and spiritual need. It is a tangible way to say, "I have done wrong and want to make that clear." The biblical phrase "to afflict oneself/one's soul" refers to fasting.[3] The repeated appearance of this term in connection with the Day of Atonement (Lev. 16:29, 31; 23:27, 32; Num. 29:7) points to the use of fasting to show recognition of sin and the need for divine mercy and forgiveness. Fasting was a way to humble oneself before God and seek His grace (Ezra 8:21; Ps. 69:10, 11).

Fasting signals times of high significance. Scripture mentions occasions such as mourning a death, celebrating a feast, or a time of national crisis. While these things may seem contradictory and cause one to wonder how the biblical writers could possibly place them together, the common theme is one of simply saying that fasting tells people, "This is an important time, and our fast marks it as such." When King Saul and his son Jonathan die, a fast is appropriate (2 Sam. 1:11, 12). During celebrations of national importance fasting takes place in the context of joy (Zech. 8:19). And when Jews learn of the decree of King Ahasuerus to slay all Jews, they naturally mourn and fast (Esther 4:1-3).

Fasting facilitates divine guidance and revelations. In several cases, Scripture mentions fasting as a part of or adjunct to prayers or worship seeking for divine guidance and revelation about issues that are unknown or mysterious. Daniel (Dan. 9:3) fasts as he attempts to understand Jeremiah's prophecy and the future fate of God's people. When the early church in Antioch fasted, the Holy Spirit instructed that they set aside Paul and Barnabas for a special task (Acts 13:2, 3) for which they then designated them by the laying on of hands. And when Paul needed to appoint leaders of his churches, the process involved fasting and prayer (Acts 14:23).

The second, third, and fourth points above seem to point out the fact that fasting adds an extra dimension to whatever it is connected with, signaling depth of feeling or meaning as well as more serious personal involvement with the issues at stake.

Fasting focuses and clarifies the mind. This purpose of fasting, and the next two as well, are not based directly on Scripture, but are common-sense truths that we should recognize. When we do something out of the ordinary, such as fast, the change in our daily life constantly reminds us that something special is happening. It focuses far more attention and thought on the reason for the fast than it would normally receive.

Closely related to this is also the physical fact that lack of food for many people sharpens the mind and thought process and brings more clarity to the issue at hand. This focus can mean greater ability to deal wisely and well with the challenge we face. "Fasting" from other things than food, such as TV, etc., can do the same thing for us.

Many receive health benefits from fasting. While certain physical conditions can preclude fasting, periodic fasting does bring health benefits for most people. Western cultures have more overfed people than underfed ones. Many European health spas promote fasting as a way to cleanse the body of accumulated toxins and purify the digestive system. You may remind me that fasting is for spiritual purposes, but we also need to remember that a healthy body facilitates spiritual growth.

Fasting creates time that we may use for spiritual purposes. Preparing food, eating it, and cleaning up afterward takes a lot of time. If during a fast we simply used the time that we would have spent with food on prayer or other ways of communion with God, we would be doing something of spiritual benefit. Fasting from shopping and entertainment has the same effect. In a world in which most have overfilled schedules, fasting can create an oasis of time for spiritual activity that may be hard to get any other way.

Guidelines for Fasting

All of these purposes help us realize that fasting can be a boon not only for our spiritual lives but also for our physical and mental ones. How do we go about practicing it in a meaningful way? I suggest here some guidelines for fasting.

Choose to fast for the right reason. You do not stack up merit or force God's hand by fasting. Look carefully at the purposes or reasons for fasting, and relate your choice to one or more of them. Ask God to give you the right motive to fast.

Consider various types of fasting. To be honest, I admit that I have a hard time with food fasts. If I go more than two mealtimes without eating, all I can think of is food, and it is hard to pray. One or two meals periodically is all that I can do. Some may not have my problem, but diabetes or other diseases may make it imperative to eat regularly. All such people would do well to think about other ways to fast.

How about a television fast, or at least a fast of one or two television shows that may not be the best to watch anyway? I have found a fast from television football to be meaningful to me. You could fast from shopping, reading the newspaper, or Internet use. The list can be almost endless. Ask God to help you find a meaningful fast that fits your situation.

Understand and know your situation. This principle follows logically on the previous point. Fasting should fit who you are spiritually, mentally, and physically. Look at your life. What is drawing you away from God or family and consuming your time? What is your besetting sin? What is your greatest spiritual need? The answers to such questions will give you insight into what would be an appropriate fast for you.

Don't fear corporate fasting. In an age of individualization most people think of fasting as a personal act. Much of the fasting in Scripture, though, was corporate- or group-oriented. We should not fear joining with others in fasting. In fact, fasting with a group is, for many, a good way to introduce themselves to the practice of fasting. The communal feeling created by doing something together makes the whole process easier and lessens the temptation to give up on the whole endeavor.

Enter the process gradually. In your enthusiasm to get started, don't plan a 40-day fast. It is probably good to start with skipping only a meal or two. For some, a partial fast of a day may work. Be gentle with yourself, and don't move on to something more until you have had success at a more modest level.

Before you do something as rigorous as a three- to seven-day fast, find out the details about what it may involve. If you have any physical questions, check with your doctor. Remember, the aim is spiritual growth and the furthering of God's kingdom, not proving you can do something or damaging your body.

Don't fast without a purpose and the inclusion of other spiritual disciplines. Fasting should occur in the context of a clear spiritual purpose. At times it can be specific—such as God's intention concerning a specific issue in your life or the life of another. It can also be as general as a desire for a renewal in one's spiritual life.

Most biblical instances of fasting clearly combine it with other spiritual disciplines, especially prayer. Fasting, in general, is more fruitful as we practice it with other spiritual practices, including prayer, meditation, worship, study, etc. Such things work together synergistically so that the result is greater than the simple sum of each part.

Don't publicize or flaunt personal fasting. Jesus is quite clear that fasting should take place in secret as much as possible and not be revealed to those outside of one's closest circle (see Matt. 6:16-18). God, not humanity, is to be the one who notices our devotion and responds to our pleas.

Conclusion

After a period of more than 100 years during which the Western church paid little attention to fasting, a renewal of interest is beginning to emerge. We have only begun to see faintly the possibilities that are there if God's people become serious about fasting. Furthermore, we have much to learn about the nature and purpose of fasting and how to practice it meaningfully. One recent attempt to go deeper is a book by Elmer Towns that suggests biblical examples illustrating nine different ways or purposes of fasting for spiritual breakthrough.[4] In an article that summarizes his book, Towns says, in conclusion:

"If every Christian fasted, the results could shake our society like a windstorm bending a sapling. By fasting, Christians would demonstrate that they live differently, that their faith is imperative, that the Almighty works in their daily lives.

"If all our churches fasted, they would move forward in evangelism, reaching out in feeding and helping others, and God would pour His presence on His people."[5]

I believe he is right, and I hope you become part of this spiritual breakthrough.

---

[1] Richard Foster, *Celebration of Discipline*, p. 47.

[2] David N. Freedman et al., eds., "Fast, Fasting," *Anchor Bible Dictionary* (New York: Doubleday, 1992), vol. 2, pp. 773-776.

[3] *Ibid.*

[4] Elmer Towns, *Fasting for Spiritual Breakthrough* (Ventura, Calif.: Regal, 1996).

[5] Elmer Towns, "Fasting for Nine Kinds of Spiritual Breakthrough," *Net Results: New Ideas in Church Vitality*, March 1999, pp. 28-30.

Chapter 9

Solitude and Simplicity

"I was pleasantly surprised on how rewarding the discipline of silence can be. It is almost as if God always wanted to say, 'Can't you shut up for a little while? I have something important to tell you.'"

"God is more real. That does not mean He was not real before, but simply because through silence, I hear Him speaking to my conscience."

—Fellow Spiritual Pilgrims

Solitude and simplicity are both ways to help get rid of the static that hampers our reception of God's communication with us. Both, properly understood and practiced, can open up the way to closer communion with God and a more religion-centered life. Solitude teaches us that a life that is so full of noise, people, and activity that it crowds out silence and time for reflection is not truly living. Simplicity tells us that a preoccupation with things and money makes us a slave to them and takes away our freedom. Problems in these areas can create situations that make spiritual progress impossible.

Solitude and Silence

For solitude, we might also use the words "silence" and "retreat." All three words imply a coming apart from normal life and a quieting of "noise." We should understand them to have both an inner and an outer quality to them.

One can outwardly retreat to a quiet place but inside bring all the normal "noise." A person can be outwardly in the hustle and bustle of life but maintain a place of solitude and quiet inside that changes everything.

Ideally, the inward and the outward can be combined and, if not happening simultaneously, at least the one can lead to the other.

Many today are lonely, and fear that solitude will increase their sense of abandonment. Others are afraid of silence, inwardly dreading what may well up within them if they really have to slow down enough to reflect on life. For still others, enforced solitude is an enemy confirming their lack of appeal to other people.

We must learn that true solitude is not loneliness but fulfillment. Solitude is not an enforced state of separation, but a choice to meet God and our true selves in a place or state in which we may most clearly hear their voices and in which refreshment of body and soul can result.

It is well for us to remember that Jesus Himself required solitude, silence, and retreat, and that He definitely believed His disciples had need of the same. My study of the gospel of Mark has driven me to see this time after time. I have referred earlier to the fact that the only place in the Gospels that seems to outline one 24-hour day in the life of Jesus is in Mark 1:21-38. He arises before dawn after ministering very late the night before. He then leaves His lodging to seek out a "lonely place" for prayer and communion with God. It makes sense, since 40 days alone in the desert had preceded His ministry (Mark 1:12, 13). Subsequent ministry reports tell us that such solitude was an ongoing practice (Mark 6:45-47). Jesus knew that His disciples needed it also (verses 31, 32). The press of people sometimes made the attempt unsuccessful (verses 33, 34 and Mark 7:24), but the necessity was evident. Do we require it any less?

Silence, as I used it earlier as a synonym for solitude, has a broad meaning of entering a place of quiet. And it is also important in its very literal, narrow meaning of not using the tongue. This is crucial in solitude because absence of speech opens us up to listening. Many of us forget the second part of Ecclesiastes 3:7: "a time to keep silence, and a time to speak" (RSV). The one who controls the tongue, the apostle James says, is a perfect person (James 3:1-12). The combination of a place apart with literal silence gives us an opportunity to hear God's voice which is otherwise squelched in our hectic lives.

Specific Benefits of Silence and Solitude

Silence and solitude play a crucial role in our spiritual life. *They remind us how much we use our words and actions to defend ourselves and to influence (ma-*

nipulate?) others. Realizing that, we can begin to relax and depend on God as our justifier and defender. We enter an area in which we can be free of thinking and planning to preserve our own reputation. Silent and alone before God, who knows all, we can truly release ourselves from all of those other attempts at self-preservation.

Silence and solitude often allow voices, needs, past wounds and hurts, as well as inner fears, etc., to surface. Our busyness and words have kept them suppressed and muted, but the solitude and silence encourage them to stand up and speak. Such an event may not be pleasant at first, but, handled properly, it can be of great benefit. Willingness to hear such voices helps us to go more deeply into self-understanding, which is related to God-understanding. The knowledge gained can remove barriers to our own healing and encourage spiritual growth. We lose in many ways if we flee solitude and silence so as to continue to suppress the voices.

Solitude and silence create space for God to speak and act. "Be still," Scripture says, "and know that I am God" (Ps. 46:10). When we silence our voice and the sounds of our environment, not only are we able to hear the repressed voices inside of us better, but God's voice can also become clearer and stronger. Silence creates a listening encounter.

Last but not least, solitude and quiet give us physical and mental rest. The stressed and hurried body and the mind filled with a thousand things and a long to-do list have a chance to slow down and rest. Thus silence and solitude heal us not only spiritually but physically and psychologically as well.

Practical Steps to Solitude

What can we do then, in a hectic life, to create periods of solitude and silence?

We can begin by planning for "mini retreats." Solitude and silence not only deal with physical apartness and literal wordlessness, but also are an attitude of mind that constantly is open to quietness in God's presence. With such a mind-set we can plan and benefit from far shorter periods of time than an extended period of one to three days.

Take advantage of the moments between when you awake and arise. If you get up to open or close windows or let the cat out when the house is still quiet, stop in silence to listen to God.

When forced to wait for children after school or in the doctor's office, use the time to relax in silence in God's presence. Or while working in your yard, stop and consider the hand of God in growing things and in the silence of wonder hear Him. Take time to silently stargaze and moon-gaze.

Create a place in your house where you can get away. It could be in an attic or basement or even a closet if you can't find a whole room. Even a section of a room or a special chair will work if you awaken before others or tell them that your presence there means you want to be silent.

Others, as Jesus did, can find a solitary place outside the home. A vacant office at work or a quiet storage area will do. A chapel or church open 24 hours will work. So will a path or wild area near home or on your driving route. Be creative, have a desire for solitude, and ask God to lead you to a place where the two of you can meet and commune together.

For a number of years I have dreamed of forming a lay missionary community. My dream includes a protocol for the spiritual life. I have tried to boil it down to the essentials. The conviction has grown in me that one of them is a yearly retreat of at least two days. Probably it would be good to do this more than once a year, but yearly is better than nothing at all.

Part of the purpose of the retreat should be to look at one's life and think deeply before God about its goals and aims for the future. Some of that time could be spent in study, but a fair portion of it should have no agenda other than to rest in God's presence and soak in His love.

Such a retreat into solitude and silence not only restores us physically, spiritually, and mentally—it also makes us more ready to relate to and to love those around us.

My hope and prayer is that more and more Christians will see this need and that more people will feel moved to create places of solitude or retreat centers to facilitate the satisfying of this hunger for solitude and silence.

Simplicity

Another way to reduce static in the human-to-God relationship is to live more simply. Simplicity brings a paradoxical spiritual freedom that liberates the spirit. People often equate it with choosing poverty over wealth. True Christian simplicity is much broader than that. It speaks not only about our money, but also our time, our talents, our relationships, and our priorities. Simplicity is more than outward action—it includes inward attitude as well. Some people of wealth cheerfully share generously with others and live simply, while others are monetarily poor but have an all-consuming desire for wealth.

Christians in the Western world particularly need the call to simplicity. For more than 30 years Ron Sider has been a persistent prophetic voice on the obligation of rich Christians to live simply so that they can share more with a hungry world. Sider observes that the real income of people in the U.S. is 14 times that of India and 17 times that of Kenya.[1] Americans spend about 13 percent of their income for food, while in India it is 55 percent and Niger 63 percent.[2] His point is simply that we are far richer than we realize and that not sharing that wealth by living simply is disobedience to the core of Christianity and a hindrance to our walk with God.

Not only does lack of simplicity hinder our relationship with God—it lessens the impact of our mission to spread Christianity. Missiologist Jonathan Bonk has written a book with the thesis that missionary affluence seriously hampers mission.[3] Missionaries' lack of simplicity encourages people to become Christians for the wrong reason (hope of wealth) and makes cross-cultural relationships challenging and missions to the poor extremely difficult.

Yet another reason simplicity is so important to us in the West is our pressure-packed lives. No one has made this clearer than author Richard Swenson in his book *Margin*.[4] Our lifestyle is so hectic that we have little room for error or change without causing major disruptions. For example, we have so little financial margin with all our monthly payments that sickness or layoff can cause serious financial problems. We are so pressed for time that two extra red lights can make us late. And we are so short on sleep that loss of a few additional hours can leave us in serious trouble. All relationships suffer, and the thought of helping others and even our family exhausts us and is often impossible. Simplicity is needed here!

We often forget how central to Scripture economic and financial issues are. The Old Testament clearly acknowledges the right to private property, but that right is subordinate to care for family or others in need.[5] One of the clearest examples of that is the jubilee (Lev. 25). Every 50 years it would redistribute land so that everyone could start over financially. The passage makes it clear that God, not individuals, is the ultimate owner of the land. As such, God does not allow people who become poor to remain so forever. The Lord created for His people an institution that assured even the poorest of an eventual fresh start and made it necessary for the richest to share.

Jesus and New Testament writers talk a lot about money and wealth and reflect the same basic idea as the Old Testament. If anything, Jesus goes further when He tells us clearly that we cannot serve both material things and God (Luke 16:13). He warns specifically that it is hard for the rich to enter the kingdom of God (Matt. 19:24). Jesus mourns when the rich young ruler chooses his possessions over giving his money away and following Him (verses 16-22). In fact, Jesus speaks more on the issue of money than on any other social topic.

If the Bible speaks so often of these issues, Christians who claim to take the Bible seriously should pay attention.

All of this said, however, we must be careful that we do not glamorize poverty and find spiritual pride in our simplicity. On the one hand we should reject any preoccupation with becoming rich. We should avoid as well what I call the Christian heresy of the health-and-wealth gospel, which says that if you truly believe in Jesus, your financial worries and poverty will disappear. I have seen too many desperately poor around the world. Many of them are more committed than most Christians I know, yet they are still poor. On the other hand, we should also reject monklike legalism that sets rules that must be followed and wears its poverty and simplicity as a badge of righteousness. Both extremes are spiritually destructive.

What helps us find our way to true Christian simplicity is our anxiety level. If we are anxious, we have simplicity problems. Whatever the issue—money, schedule, work, family—anxiety tips us off to problems. If we make God's kingdom first in our lives, we can be free of anxiety and live in true simplicity.

By doing so, we will find our lives characterized by three inner attitudes.[6] First, we will consider what we have—money, possessions, time, family, etc.—as a gift from God and not something that we created. Second, we will regard all of these things as cared for by God, and our care is only secondary. Third, what we have will be available to others. When such attitudes pervade our lives, we will begin to experience the freedom that true simplicity brings.

Practical Suggestions

For more than two decades I have been in close contact with college and university students as professor, mentor, and friend. Two major issues in many of their lives especially challenge their ability to live lives of true simplicity. (And many who are not students face similar difficulties.)

The first is debt. Long before graduation and the first postcollege job, the enticement to use consumer credit begins. Opportunities to acquire credit cards flood dormitory mailboxes. The credit companies offer all kinds of "incentives" for students to sign up, and many succumb. I have counseled graduate students who owe thousands in credit card debt and whose monthly payments go 90 percent to interest. Add to this car payments—often on a vehicle that is more than they need—furniture, and appliances bought on time, and the load is heavy. Financial worries, time pressures, extra jobs needed to pay bills, etc., all follow, and the cycle of debt with its ugly results becomes firmly established. I tell people that this is a spiritual issue. True, it is related to finances, but at heart it is a spiritual problem. The debt cycle not only brings stress and anxiety but crowds out time that they should spend on family, friends, service to others, and devotion to God. "Owe no one anything, except to love one another," says Romans 13:8 (RSV). We need to recall the literal truth of Proverbs 22:7: "The borrower is servant to the lender." Sad to say, even some of us at Christian colleges have too easily allowed students to run up excessive educational debt.

All Christian colleges require religion courses. I believe that the curriculum should include a course that teaches Christian stewardship and simplicity and warns students about what debt slavery can do to them.

The second major enemy to simplicity that I see rampant today is the computer and video revolution. I refer not only to television and the computer, but also to all the new gadgets that people use to view movies, listen to music, play games, surf the Web, etc. The addictions and preoccupations that arise from them are many. Some, such as pornography, are demonic or even illegal. Others, such as soap operas and sports, may not in themselves be sinful but can easily be huge time wasters. For some students, computer games consume as much or more time than actual study. Many even become "knowledge junkies" and spend hours on Web research that bears little real-life fruit. All of these things can happen almost imperceptibly in our lives and then consume large amounts of time. They take time from things that we really need to do and must then neglect or perform hastily. Again, we must say that this is a spiritual issue, not just an efficiency matter. Many of these things do literally become hard-to-break addictions that rob us of our freedom like any habit-forming drug.

In conclusion, I hold out to you the freeing vision of Jesus in Matthew 6:25-34. He tells us not to be anxious about anything—food, drink, clothes, money, etc. It will do us no good, He says. God knows our needs. If we make His kingdom first, we will have all these things as gifts from Him. The true freedom many seek can be ours as we listen to Jesus' voice and begin to practice solitude and simplicity.

---

[1] Ron Sider, *Rich Christians in an Age of Hunger* (Downers Grove: InterVarsity Press, 1984), p. 33.

[2] *Ibid.*, p. 35.

[3] Jonathan Bonk, *Missions and Money: Affluence as a Western Missionary Problem* (Maryknoll, N.Y.: Orbis Press, 1991).

[4] Richard Swenson, *Margin* (Colorado Springs, Colo.: NavPress, 1992).

[5] Sider, p. 103.

[6] Richard Foster, *Celebration of Discipline*, p. 88.

Chapter 10

Why No Urgency?

"I have come to realize that spiritual formation is the heart of being a Christian."

"Not only is He [God] good, He is more real than I thought Him to be. He is real when I pray."

—Fellow Spiritual Pilgrims

Posing the Question

Some people have doubts about the reality of the spiritual life. They wonder if worship and prayer really do anything or make a difference. Others may even intellectually agree with the suggestions of this book but sense no urgency to practice the life of communion with God. Can they really meet God? We should take such questions seriously, because they represent deeply held concepts and attitudes that we need to address if the spiritual life is to prosper. I believe that the best way to deal with these issues is to examine the concept of religious worldview. It confronts the core question as to whether God works in everyday life and if so in what ways.

Our culture and view of life in general influence our spiritual life or the lack thereof. Few realize how much past events plus deep ideas and concepts that we often cannot even express will shape our life. Anthropologists call one aspect of this deep influence "worldview." In this chapter we explore how worldview heavily affects our beliefs and practices (or lack of practices) in the area of the spiritual life. Whether we pray or not, how we pray, what we pray about, as well as all our devotional practices all profoundly reflect our worldview.

What Is Worldview?

We can define worldview as the deep, underlying, usually unconscious concept structures of a people or culture that is the source for their values, beliefs, and actions. Although at times various writers use different terms, we can suggest that human thought and action have four layers that function like an inverted pyramid (see Figure 1). At the bottom, the smallest segment of the pyramid is worldview. It is small because it has fewer elements, i.e., basic concepts, yet it serves as the source from which all other layers emerge. Going up, the next layer is values. Worldview gives rise to values that label things as good or bad, helpful or harmful. Developing out of these values are concepts (the third level) that tell us what thoughts we should believe in based on consistency with our values and worldview. The largest and top portion of the inverted pyramid is the multitude of our actions and behavior. They arise from the beliefs we hold that in turn have been given birth to by our values and worldview.

Let me offer a simple illustration of how this works. Yesterday my graduate students came to class on time—at least they tried. Their behavior stemmed from the conviction that they would do better in school if they got to class before it started, a belief based on the value that it is a good thing to succeed in school and get high grades. Underlying it all is the worldview that accepts the validity of the schooling system. That worldview gives rise to all kinds of behavior, beliefs, and values aimed at helping the student get into school, stay in school, and successfully graduate.

Also underlying such "on time to class" behavior are beliefs, values, and a worldview related to time. The belief is that it is proper, polite, and respectful to be on time. The value underneath that is that it is a good thing to use time well and a bad thing to waste or misuse it. At the deepest worldview level this stems from the idea that our time is finite (we have only a limited amount), linear (not cyclical), and measurable. Such worldview ideas rarely get discussed or even recognized, but they are the source of all behaviors. Few are aware that other cultures and other intellectual eras hold differing basic views of time. We assume that all others have the same basic views as we do, because for us they are *the* way to do things.

Implications for Religious Life

All this has wide ramifications in the spiritual realm. One of the basic worldview issues is the activity (or nonactivity) of God in everyday life. Can one actually encounter God in the spiritual disciplines, such as prayer, meditation, worship, etc.? If we see God as truly touching human life in such practices, our incentive or urge to perform them has great meaning and power. But if we believe that such activities have more to do with my inner psychological issues and/or that God does not normally meet people in daily life, the strong motivation to practice the disciplines disappears. Few of us spend time on things that our worldview tells us are unimportant or marginally productive. Many modern people, even Christians, at the deepest worldview level do not believe that God is active in everyday life. No wonder the practice of the spiritual life has suffered in Western culture!

I have been greatly helped in my understanding of this issue by an article written by Paul Hiebert entitled "The Flaw of the Excluded Middle" that I have developed, and used in some new ways. Although Hiebert's original intention was to find a way for Western missionaries to address the issues of spirits, ancestors, astrology, healing, etc., in non-Western cultures, I think that we can apply his concepts to the question of the spiritual life as well. His article gives us a way to think systematically and to visualize the issues.[1]

Hiebert suggests a six-segment three-level diagram that is an analysis of religious worldview systems (see Figure 2). His argument is that mainstream Western culture, because of its rational enlightenment view of the universe, sees the world as a closed system that we can understand almost completely at the lower human empirical level. Western science in both its social science branch (psychology, anthropology, etc.) and physical science forms (biology, physics, chemistry, zoology, etc.) operate on the basis of the bottom level in the diagram. Even Western Christians who, because of their belief in God, accept the upper or divine level of the chart often have trouble believing in the middle level of the diagram. Culture and education reflect the enlightenment worldview that subtly but with constant pressure questions the reality and validity of the middle level. Thus the title, "Excluded Middle," for Hiebert's article. Western enlightenment culture tends to forget, exclude, or not utilize the whole middle area of the diagram.

The middle level is the means of communication between the upper and lower levels. Ignoring that area seriously hampers the interchange between top and bottom levels. Communion or communication with God does not then happen.

The ramifications are many. For one thing, it affects communication between cultures. A culture that believes in spirits and demons has trouble understanding one that doesn't. It also shapes how we understand the Bible. Do we regard statements or stories that involve the middle level as true or literal? Even a cursory reading of the Bible suggests that it commonly accepts elements in this middle area. Morton Kelsey in his book *Encounter With God*[2] suggests that 49 percent of the New Testament deals with the middle area of experience. If, however, we don't take it seriously, how do we interpret the Bible?

Most important for our consideration is how this all affects the spiritual life. Do the spiritual disciplines really put us into contact with the divine or not? The traditional enlightenment Western worldview with its excluded middle questions any divine activity in life and subtly undermines the cruciality and value of the spiritual life. I would suggest it is this worldview that has affected many of the things discussed in chapter 1, such as our definitions of religion and theology.

Using this basic six-part religious worldview diagram, I suggest there exist at least five basic worldview options (note Figures 3-7). I have circled the parts of the worldview diagram accepted by each particular worldview. These five options help us understand how one's worldview leads to various perspectives on the spiritual life.

The first is *atheistic/agnostic* (Figure 3). Its adherents accept only the bottom level of the diagram, the human empirical. God is nonexistent or irrelevant. Seeing the world as a closed system understandable by the scientific method means that they do not recognize or need any divine presence or activity. In the absence of the divine, there is no spiritual life.

The second worldview is *deist* (Figure 4). The deist believes in the top and bottom levels of the diagram. God is the creator and maker of the laws of the universe but rarely intervenes. The cosmic watchmaker who made the world to operate like a watch and then wound it up, He has given certain laws or principles that we learn and operate by, so that neither the universe nor humanity need any personal, regular, hands-on supervision.

Many Christians, especially intellectuals in midlife or older, are really closet deists. They find difficulty with things such as biblical miracles, intercessory prayer, or anything that suggests God's direct action in the world. Their tendency also is to take things that the Bible would place in the middle area and, by redefining them, bump them down to the bottom level. An illustration would be giving lip service to prayer, but defining it in a solely psychological sense of putting our minds or lives in line with God's will. Another example would be defining all personal demonic encounters in terms of mental illness or emotional abnormalities. Some would even regard the Bible as a basically human book. Anyone trained in a Western cultural setting, even in Christian schools, has imbibed much of the deist worldview.

The third possible worldview option is the *magical* (see Figure 5). Here we must understand "magic" in its anthropological sense. We are not talking about sleight of hand and visual illusions of the Houdini type. Rather, magic means the art of controlling or manipulating events by supernatural power. To those who practice magic, it is a science in the sense that it operates by laws and principles that the practitioner understands and uses. The magical worldview believes completely in the right side of the diagram. The challenges of relating to a personal deity give way to the predictability of divine mechanical operation. We see this operating in the use of spells, chants, and magical words that supposedly guarantee specific blessings or curses. The use of amulets to provide protection operates on the same concept. And we find it among Christians who are always searching for the right formula or the specific steps to some spiritual or personal goal. If they can just claim some specific promise, God will act.

Such people believe in what I call the "Coke machine" deity. God operates like a soft drink vending machine. If you just put in the right coins, out comes a drink. The magical view of God claims that all you have to do is say the right words or do the right thing, and He is obligated to deliver the goods.

The fourth possible worldview, the *medieval/mystical* (see Figure 6), accepts and lives by the top two layers of the diagram and questions the bottom one. Those who objected to Ben Franklin's invention of the lightning rod reflect this viewpoint. They thought it was wrong, because humans were playing with "God's artillery." Christians or others who see all disease or physical problems as related to God or other spiritual powers also reflect such a perspective. Nutrition, health principles, and physical habits such as smoking are irrelevant. You simply pray or perform the right religious ritual, and sickness will disappear. Because the laws of nature are all direct acts of God, those who hold such a view question the physical sciences.

The fifth worldview I have called the *Christian theist* (see Figure 7). Accepting the whole diagram and keeping it in balance, it believes that God and the laws of the universe both exist at the top level. Both sides of the chart have validity. They believe that true divine-human interchange takes place (middle level), and that God has made an orderly world in which He expects us to live responsibly (lower level). In reality a true version of this chart should not have rigid boundaries between the levels and the two sides. The boundaries between areas are fluid, and the various areas interpenetrate.

Clearly I believe that all worldviews but the last one are inadequate. Truncated, they see only part of the world. Their worldview lens allows them to see only part of the whole.

Implications for the Spiritual Life

Even more important than the fact that the first four worldviews are incomplete is the fact that they give an inadequate basis for the spiritual life.

An atheistic worldview has no basis for interaction with God, while a deist worldview believes in God but limits His ability to interface with people. Special revelation, prayer, and worship must all be defined in a limited sense. The magical worldview turns God into an automaton. Religion becomes the search for the magical formula. The personal side of God and any idea of mystery thus vanish. The medieval/mystical view, on the other hand, makes God capricious and downplays the role of the physical world that He has created, depriving life of a sense of order and structure of law.

The rise of modern science and the empirical worldview during the past 100 years has radically affected the world—especially Western society and educated people. For it the politically correct worldview is one that believes in a closed system, thus automatically pushing one to the atheistic or agnostic worldview. At best it would accept the deist perspective, which does believe in God, albeit a distant nonactive one. As we have noted, many educated Christians are closet deists. They have a difficult time believing in prayer, worship, and revelation because they have, often unconsciously, drunk so deeply of the scientific worldview. Thus the world today questions divine activity at a deep, often unconscious level. The spiritual then loses importance and priority because it has had its whole underlying basis destroyed. Why is prayer crucial—other than changing me—if God is not at work in the world? Why put a priority on doing things that don't make any difference?

Changing Our Worldview

For spirituality to flourish, we must return to a Christian theistic worldview. How can we foster that? Such transformation comes gradually, but a simple recognition of the problem and a desire to change helps the process begin. I always suggest to people that they start to pray and act *as if* God could work in the world today, and as He reveals Himself, things will take place.

Living for a while with people who have a different worldview can help. Even a short mission trip to another culture can alter one's perspective. For me living in Asia among animist and Buddhist people who believed in the everyday activity of the supernatural enabled me to see my own outlook more clearly and to recognize the need for a worldview adjustment.

But, you may ask, how do we know that the fifth worldview (figure 7) is true? For Christians the basic answer is that it is a core teaching of the Bible. In the Old Testament key characters have interaction with God. Adam and Eve walk and talk with Him, as do Abraham and Moses. God communicated directly with prophets in words, visions, and dreams. He responded to prayers through divine action. The core underlying assumption is that He reveals Himself and His works in the arena of human life.

Jesus is the center of the New Testament. His coming in the Incarnation as a human baby is the ultimate expression of divine presence in human life and history. God is literally with us in the form of Jesus. Even after Christ leaves, the story of the early church is that He sends the Holy Spirit as His active messenger in the world, and the church grows because God is present and active. The fact that He answers prayer and changes human lives is a New Testament teaching at the most basic of levels.

For those who are nonbelievers I simply challenge them to try to see if God works. Do an experiment—a scientific lab experiment. Simply say, "God, I'm not sure You really want to act in my life, but I want to be open to it." You may even admit, "God, I don't know if You even exist, but I'd really like to honestly give You a chance to show Yourself. If You want to be active in my life, please reveal that to me." It is better if you request no specific response, but that you leave it open for God to act in whatever way *He* desires. Then be alert and observant. I believe God responds to people who sincerely desire to know Him. Be prepared to change your worldview! Try practicing the spiritual habits mentioned in this book. Be honest, and by these or other actions create a space for God to act. I believe that He will.

In conclusion, I emphasize that if God really intervenes in human life, then the devotional life becomes the number one priority in a believer's experience. When God shows up, then He will satisfy our hunger for Him. The devotional life is the way that contact and communication with an active God takes place. Who wants to go through life muddling along on their own when divine presence, guidance, and help is available?

One of my professors once said, "The sign of an educated person is that they recognize the implications of what they believe." If you really accept that God works in peoples' lives, then the clear implication is that keeping in regular dynamic contact with Him becomes the top priority. Spiritual formation and the devotional life assume life's highest priority, and contact with God empowers and influences all that we do.

Figure 1.

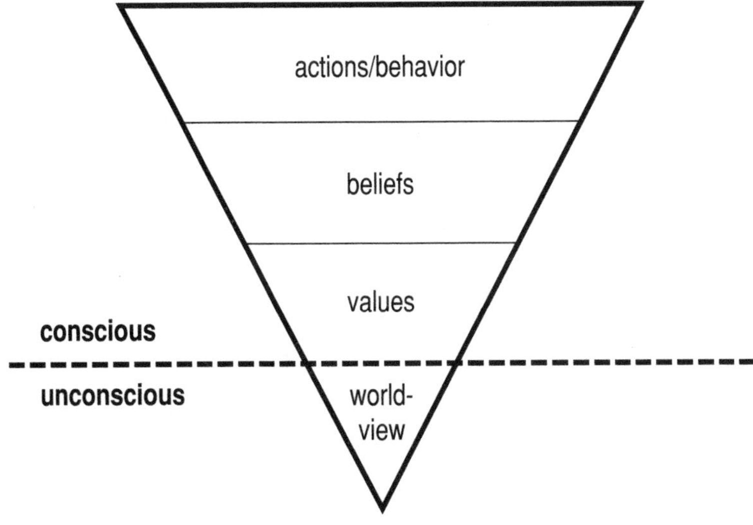

Figure 2. Analysis of Religious Worldview

	Organic/Personal	Mechanical/Impersonal
divine unseen	personal God Satan high God	karma fate brahman cosmic forces
middle	healers prophets demons angels ghosts spirits, etc.	magic astrology charms, amulets, etc. meditation prayer, etc. dreams, visions Bible
human empirical	social sciences human relations animals	natural sciences physical and mechanical sciences

Figure 3. Atheistic/Agnostic

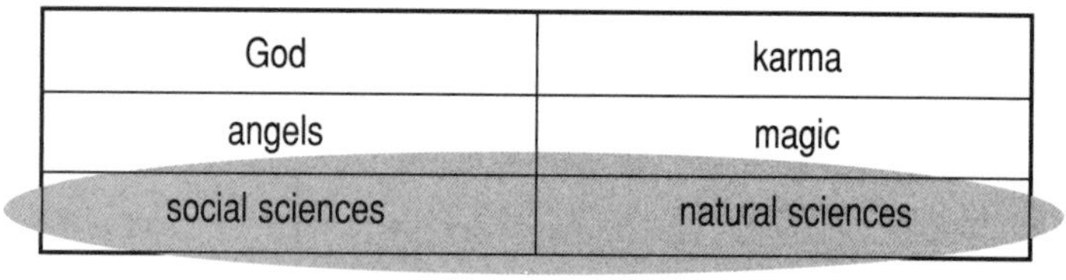

God	karma
angels	magic
social sciences	natural sciences

Figure 4. Deist

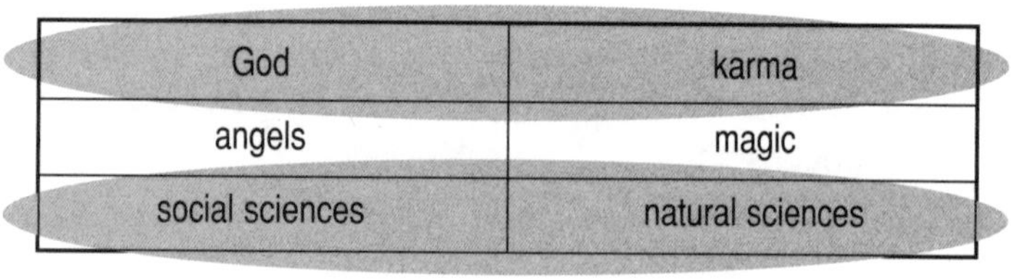

God	karma
angels	magic
social sciences	natural sciences

Figure 5. **Magical**

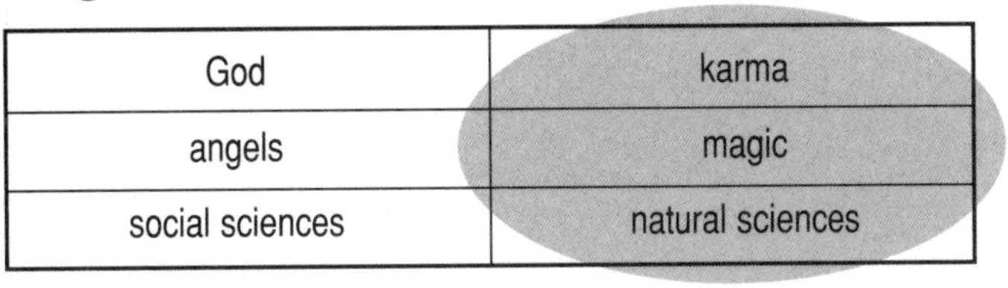

God	karma
angels	magic
social sciences	natural sciences

Figure 6. **Medieval/Mystic**

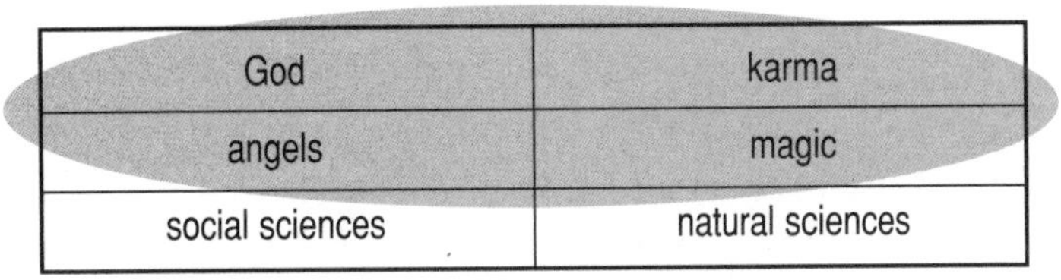

God	karma
angels	magic
social sciences	natural sciences

Figure 7. **Christian Theist**

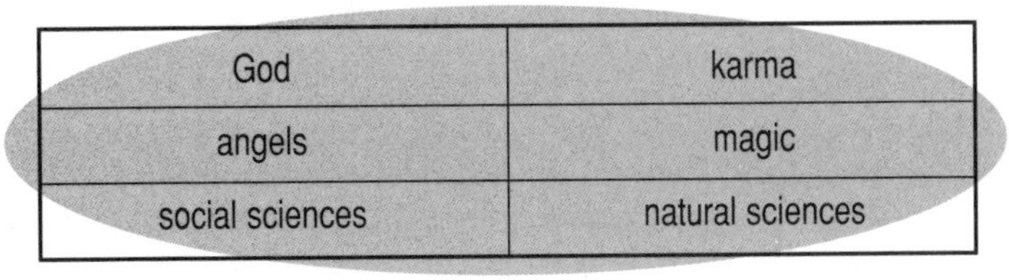

God	karma
angels	magic
social sciences	natural sciences

[1] Paul G. Hiebert, "The Flaw of the Excluded Middle," *Missiology: An International Review* 10, no. 1 (January 1982): 35-47.

[2] Morton Kelsey, *Encounter With God* (Minneapolis: Bethany Fellowship, 1972), p. 242.

Chapter 11

Why Is My Experience Different?

"I was convicted . . . that it is the things I am scared about that control me."

"Learning to accept who I was made it a lot easier to present myself to the one who takes me as I am."

—Fellow Spiritual Pilgrims

Posing the Question

Invariably we compare ourselves with other people. But when we do so, it becomes obvious that we all respond differently to spiritual things. What powerfully impacts me may leave you unmoved. You may enjoy meditation while I may struggle with it. Preferred worship styles differ widely. Why is this so? The present chapter seeks to answer this question.

It is easy to forget that self-knowledge and God-knowledge go and grow together. The more we know ourselves, the more clearly we can trace the hand of God in our lives. Lack of self-knowledge and, in particular, self-deception are real barriers to the spiritual life. For that reason we need to begin to ask questions about ourselves at the same time we try to learn more about relating to God. We can here only begin to scratch the surface of what that means. Most people enjoy finding out more about themselves, so I invite you to take that pleasant journey now.

Three aspects of self-knowledge concern us here. The first is personal temperament—we study what specific dispositions we as individuals possess. Second is our church style or tradition. Various religious traditions have different ways of practicing religion and the spiritual life, and that dramatically affects us. The third aspect is our unique cultural and psychological history that touches everything that we think and do.

Before we begin our journey, we need to take note of some cautions. I suggest four of them.

The following analyses are not precise. We must be careful not to pigeonhole ourselves or others by fixing a label. Whether that label is a temperament, religious tradition, or cultural background, it can be only partly correct. All classifications have varying degrees, and all people are unique combinations. Temperament types are usually true in broad outline, but are, at best, only a partial picture of a complex person.

Don't use personal analysis as a reason for laziness or wrong behavior. Employing a temperament or a cultural or psychological wound to excuse inaction or improper action is a misuse of knowledge and not helpful.

Realize that no one spiritual path works for everyone. We are all different, and not only should we be open to new ways of relating to God based on the person He made us—we should allow and encourage others to do the same.

4. *God has provided ways for all people to relate to Him and be comfortable in doing so.* No temperament type or religious tradition or psychological condition can force one to say, "God left me out." True spiritual formation has such a variety of ways to reach out to Him that everyone can find something that fits the way He made them.

Personal Temperament

Christian circles have widely used two particular temperament tests.[1] The first is the four-temperament theory that sees most people as varying blends of usually two of four types of temperament: choleric (bold, aggressive, energetic); sanguine (sociable, disorganized, cheerful); melancholy (emotional, creative, moody); and phlegmatic (calm, easygoing, flexible).

Although the basic concept has existed since the early Greeks (Aristotle discussed it), the British psychologist Hans Eysenck has done the most research on it.[2] Best-selling author Tim LaHaye, beginning in the 1970s, popularized a test based on the theory.[3]

While this four-temperament test can be helpful, for spiritual formation purposes I prefer the second test—some form of the Myers-Briggs

Type Indicator (MBTI). The MBTI has more depth and does not lend itself quite as easily to quick labeling. Another reason is that many religious counselors have employed the MBTI in spiritual formation. The test has become the most widely used personality assessment in the world.[4]

A mother-daughter team devised the Myers-Briggs test. They worked for years using psychologist Carl Jung's book *Psychological Types* as a theoretical basis. The test made an immediate impact after its publication in 1975.

If you have not undergone the assessment or have forgotten the four letters that show your temperament preferences, I suggest you do one of the following things. First, seek out someone who is an accredited administrator of the test and take it. As a second option, buy a book such as *Please Understand Me,* by David Keirsey and Marilyn Bates[5] and use the simplified MBTI found in the book. Better yet, read the book and get a broad introduction to the application of the test. The third option is to procure the book *Knowing Me, Knowing God,*[6] by Malcolm Goldsmith, and employ the altered form of the MBTI found there. This adaption of the MBTI couches all questions in a religious context. Various sites in the Internet also offer the test.

The theory behind the MBTI is that all of us are born with innate preferences. They affect the way we perceive the world around us, take in information, process it, and develop our responses to it. In the same way, those innate preferences affect our relationship with people and the world by affecting how we relate to God and practice our religion. Such preferences and actions are largely unconscious. We practice them naturally because they are part of who we are.

What follows is a very brief and simplified explanation of the various preferences and an attempt to begin to apply them to the spiritual life.

The first letter in the MBTI test result is either an E or an I.[7] The E stands for "extrovert" and I for "introvert." Often people misunderstand this scale, because most assume extroverts are outgoing and sociable while introverts are shy and retiring. The scale on the MBTI speaks rather to where and how a person is energized. Extroverts *gain* energy by being with people, while introverts *lose* energy in contact with people. Extroverts go home from social occasions energized, while introverts come home drained.

Most extroverts find prayer more difficult, while introverts find it relatively easier.[8] And most extroverts experience corporate prayer with others as easier than private prayer, while for many introverts the opposite is true—especially if expected to pray aloud in the presence of others. For extroverts a silent retreat may be oppressive, while the introvert takes to it like a duck to water. Extroverted spirituality needs to engage the world, while introverted spirituality treasures the inner journey on a private path to God. Most devotional books have introverts as authors (as are most books on spirituality—including this one!), and Christian churches tend to favor that type of spirituality. In North American society extroverts outnumber introverts by two to one. Introverts, beware—make your church especially inviting to introverts, and you are neglecting two thirds of your potential audience.

The second preference scale on the MBTI is either N (iNtuitive) or S (sensing). Intuitives look at the big picture and are future-oriented. They seek to transform the world and are always searching for a better way, particularly in a conceptual sense. On the other hand, taking in information through their senses, sensers are in tune with the real world. Sensers are concerned with the here and now and its details, while intuitives are bored with details. In North America 75 percent of the population are sensers, but the percentage of intuitives in the church is much larger than in the general population. Religious leaders tend to be intuitives.

Sensers like spirituality to be simple—not wordy, theoretical, and complex. Intuitives are into possibilities, questions, and mystery. While sensers like to pray concretely, with attention to specific detail, intuitives tend toward general prayer. Sensers are aware of their bodies and the world in an engaged way, whereas intuitives seem to be more fascinated by ideas about such things. Finally, sensers would like to do things for God, while intuitives are pleased thinking thoughts about Him.

On the MBTI the third preference scale is either F (feeling) or T (thinking). This does not mean that feelers do not think and thinkers are void of feeling. It simply indicates that when we must decide between going with our emotions or our logic, we demonstrate our temperament. While in general society about 60 percent of women and about 40 percent of men are feelers, the church by its very nature tends to attract feelers. Preliminary figures suggest that in churches feelers outnumber thinkers three to one.[9]

Feelers tend to form decisions that primarily take people into account, while thinkers would make those same decisions based on principles of justice or integrity.

In the spiritual realm feelers emphasize God as personal and identify easily with Bible images and stories. They sense religious atmosphere and have a "feel" for the response of a congregation and for the flow of a worship service. Religious practice that is too cognitive disturbs feelers. Thinkers, on the other hand, like to emphasize God as righteous, just, faithful, and reasonable. As a general characteristic they like to be logical, cool, and analytical. For thinkers the process of analyzing religion can be a spiritual exercise. Because many churches have a tendency to be predominately "feeling" places, the minority thinkers, especially female thinkers who also fight a gender stereotype, often feel marginalized.

The fourth of the MBTI preference scales is either J (judging) or P (perceiving). The two-word descriptions can be misleading. J's are not necessarily judgmental about people or situations—rather they are people who like structure. They like to know ahead of time what is supposed to happen, and then they want to see it take place according to that plan. J's like order and completion. P's are open to many different paths, appreciate flexibility and spontaneity, and can live more easily with ambiguity. Structuring a P is difficult, while doing something at the last minute disturbs a J.

J's have an easier time scheduling and following a regular devotional time, while P's are challenged by that practice. Someone has said that monastic life with its fairly rigid structure was designed specifically for P's who need the schedule to get their lives in order! P's tend to be more open to religious experimentation, while J's like to keep on doing what is already structured. J's usually come to decisions more quickly so they can avoid ambiguity, while P's will take time to consider things more deeply, undisturbed by the lengthening period of indecision.

We could say much, much more about all the temperament preferences, but this gives at least some idea of certain implications for our spiritual lives. I urge those interested to study further.

Faith Tradition

To even the casual observer, the spiritual life taking place at a traditional Catholic church is quite different from that at a storefront Pentecostal meeting place. The particular faith tradition we espouse affects not only the corporate worship we experience, but the personal spiritual life as well. One author who has tried to systematize this concept and apply it is James Bryan Smith. He suggests six different spiritual life traditions or emphases.[10] While others undoubtedly may classify them differently, I find his helpful and outline them below. The various traditions do not refer to specific denominations. While in some denominations two or three traditions may predominate, most large branches of Christianity have people in most or all of the traditions.

1. *The Contemplative Movement* emphasizes intimacy with God, often in a setting apart from the busyness and possibly sinful life of the world. Meditation, quietness, and contemplative prayer are hallmarks of the tradition.

2. *The Holiness Tradition.* Particularly associated with the early Methodism of John and Charles Wesley, this spirituality clearly recognizes the moral laxity of the world and finds all the ways it can to overcome sinful habits and promote an upright moral life.

3. *The Charismatic Tradition* emphasizes the active role of the Holy Spirit in the life of the believer. The presence and gifts of the Spirit, fervent prayer, and anointed worship propel evangelism and empower lives.

4. *Social Justice Tradition.* Drawing on the social justice emphasis of the biblical prophets and the compassion toward people of Jesus, this tradition sees the spiritual life as devoting one's self to helping others in need. The spiritual life is what gives rise to and nurtures care for others.

5. *Evangelical Tradition.* Stressing the seriousness of the call to share the gospel message with others, it focuses all spiritual life on preparation for and participation in the great task that Jesus gave to the church.

6. *The Incarnational Tradition.* Viewing the Christian life as a wholistic commitment affecting all of life, it sees family, daily duties, and prayer as all working as a unified whole to incarnate the presence of God into all of existence.

As one considers this list, it becomes clear that few, if any, people live completely within one tradition. We all are blended creatures that combine elements of more than one stream. No one size fits all. The fact is, however, that most have one or two traditions that they tend to reflect in their lives. This is, in fact, good simply because all six traditions have elements of truth in them. People who emphasize the various traditions remind us of that and help keep us balanced. What is important is that we do not go to extremes within our tradition. The social justice activist cannot deny the need for personal holiness and prayer. The contemplative should not neglect ministry in the world. The holiness tradition followers must not forget the call to share their faith with others.

We must also be careful not to belittle or denigrate traditions or emphases different from our own. The body of Christ profits from all traditions, and we must celebrate them in others, not mourning the fact that they are different from us, but rejoicing in the variety of God's gifts to His church.

Cultural and Psychological Background

The third element in discovering who we are before God is the cultural and psychological background we bring to the divine-human relationship. One could write volumes on this, but I give just a brief introduction to stir up some connections in our minds that will undoubtedly grow as we practice the specifics of the spiritual disciplines.

In teaching spiritual formation to culturally diverse classes, I find one huge area in which culture affects how we view the spiritual disciplines. That is the difference between individualistic societies, such as America and Western Europe, and more communal societies, often found in Africa and Asia. Individualistic Westerners regard the deepest spiritual life primarily as a private matter. Deep communion happens, they believe, through *personal* study, prayer, and contemplation of nature *by one's self.* For the communal society, the deepest religious experience happens *with others*–if not in corporate worship, at least in a family sense. Study is discussion with others, prayer is group prayer, and even contemplation may happen best with fellow believers. Some cultures are quiet when they are most deeply moved, while others want a noisy celebration. Sensitivity to this issue helps us understand ourselves and others better.

Our psychological and emotional history also affects how we relate to God. Once while riding on a bus between Los Angeles and the Pacific Northwest, I fell into conversation with a young woman who worked as a nightclub host in Las Vegas. We conversed about many issues, but finally, when she found out that I taught religion, talk turned to God. She knew little about Christianity, so I began to share the message of Jesus with her. I happened to tell her that Christ said that God is like a caring father. Eyes flashing, Lucy exploded. "If God is anything like my father," she said, "I want nothing to do with Him!" She poured out a story of lifelong criticism, rejection, and obvious lack of love. According to her, she had experienced that rejection anew that very day, just before she boarded the bus. Lucy's history of family abuse affected her spiritual perception.

While your story may not be as dramatic as Lucy's, your family and emotional history seriously impacts your religious life. How important people in your life have treated you subtly but strongly shapes both your response to God and your spiritual life. Some need to work on healing these wounds of the past so that they can relate realistically to God. Most (all?) would benefit in their spiritual life by recognizing the ways their emotional history still drives them today. A spiritual psychological profile would help most of us relate more realistically to God and our own devotional life.

Who are we, God? We are incredibly diverse, unique, complex people whom You deeply love. The more we understand what this means—for ourselves and others—the better prepared we are able to realize why our spiritual life is different from that of others . Once we have realized that, we can then respond and relate to a caring God in healthy ways.

---

[1] A third test has also had some circulation—especially, it seems, among Roman Catholics. Called the Enneagram, it has nine different basic temperament types. For details, see Renee Baron and Elizabeth Wagele, *The Enneagram Made Easy* (New York: HarperCollins, 1994), and Andreas Ebert and Marion Küstenmacher, eds., *Experiencing the Enneagram* (New York: Crossroad, 1992).

[2] See Peter Blitchington and Robert J. Cruise, *Understanding Your Temperament* (Berrien Springs, Mich.: Andrews University Press, 1979), p. 15.

[3] See, for example, Tim LaHaye, *Understanding the Male Temperament* (Old Tappan, N.J.: Revell, 1977).

[4] Malcolm Goldsmith, *Knowing Me, Knowing God* (Nashville: Abingdon, 1997), p. 22.

[5] David Keirsey and Marilyn Bates, *Please Understand Me: Character and Temperament Types* (Gnosology Books, 1984). Distributed by Prometheus Nemesis Book Co., P.O. Box 2748, Del Mar, California 92014.

[6] See note 4.

[7] Actually the letter could be an X, which some use to indicate that the test shows that the person is exactly in the middle of the E-I scale.

[8] In many of my spiritual discipline applications I am indebted to Malcolm Goldsmith.

[9] Goldsmith, p. 72.

[10] James Bryan Smith, with Linda Graybeal, *A Spiritual Formation Workbook*, rev. ed. (New York: HarperCollins, 1999). Smith thanks Richard Foster for his concept of the six traditions.

Chapter 12

Are Spiritual Practices Legalistic?

"I believed for a long time that when one is devoted to a relationship with Christ that your life has to be 'close to perfection,' but I am glad that God has delivered me from this erroneous belief. . . . I have come to understand that even in my weakness, God still meets me at the place I have committed to meet Him."

"I have enjoyed being forced to get real with my devotional life."

"It is paradoxical to me to realize that the more time I set apart for devotion, the more time I have for other things."

—Fellow Spiritual Pilgrims

Posing the Question

When I teach spiritual formation to students, part of their assignment consists of required devotional time. I ask them to log three and a half hours of any type of personal devotion spread over a minimum of four days each week. At the end of the week they must turn in a one-page report about it. Inevitably some protest. Such a reporting and keeping of time, they say, is artificial and legalistic, and destroys spiritual spontaneity. To be spiritual, they believe, means that the devotional life must be free, unscheduled, and unreported.

I point out that noting the time at the beginning and end should not really hurt spontaneity. Also I remind them that I give them lots of time flexibility and a wide choice of what they do during it. They are free to read devotionally, sit silently, meditate, listen to music that speaks to them spiritually, pray, draw, walk in nature, or any other activity that connects them with God. In the end, most find it to be a good experience. Many who initially protested soon find that the practice of reporting reveals the painful reality of how little time they have been spending with God. In the end most are thankful for the structure.

The question the students raise, however, is a valid one and in a broader sense very important. Legalistic Christians can turn the spiritual disciplines into a death-dealing law. Regular devotional time can become a way of working your way into heaven and of seeking God's favor. If, however, the practice of the spiritual life manifests a heart seeking after God and inner as well as outer transformation, the disciplines become a joy-filled process resulting in freedom. The present chapter seeks to spell out how and why this is true.

Grace and Human Effort

Some perceptive students ask a related question on an even deeper level. Is not salvation by grace alone the free gift of God? If that is the case, can spiritual devotional disciplines done by us contribute to this salvation? To express it another way, if we have been by faith freely put right with God through Jesus' actions for us, do we then move on to a holy life created by our own works of devotion? Are we justified and made right with God by faith but sanctified or made holy by our works, including our devotional practice? Richard Foster answers this question succinctly when he comments, "The analysis is correct—human striving *is* insufficient and righteousness *is* a gift from God—but the conclusion is faulty. Happily there is something we can do."[1]

What Foster is saying is that justification and sanctification are by faith because both are the work of God. To conclude from this, however, that we can't or shouldn't do anything is not correct. The something we can do is the spiritual disciplines. They put us in the presence of God where He can by His grace and power remake and revive us. Such disciplines, rightly understood, are a "means of . . . grace"[2] that God uses to work in us by His power. No amount of spiritual practice can save us—only God can. If, however, we fail to commune with Him and relate to Him through the path of the disciplines, our experience of grace and love soon wanes as does that of any relationship without constant nurture.

My favorite word picture for the role of the spiritual disciplines comes from the title of a book about the spiritual life by Donald Postema: *Space for God*.[3] The disciplines literally create room for Him to work. I see in my mind's eye my life as a cluttered, too-full room. A multitude of voices clamor for my time and effort. The room is full of so many pieces of furniture and boxes that I often stumble or am tripped up as I struggle to respond. New demands pile boxes on top of boxes and add new trinkets. Good things take the place of the best, and God gets crowded out of the room. But the spiritual disciplines create a space in that crowded room for Him to enter, be present, and work. Some boxes are removed or organized and trinkets get trashed. I make "space" for God and me to meet. The greater the space I create for Him, the more far reaching His influence and the more order and meaning that pervade the room. He does all the work—we simply clear a space for Him to accomplish it. Grace is God in action, while the spiritual disciplines provide room for it to happen.

Amazingly, this is literally true. I had a busy professional woman visit me and say, "I'd like to meet God. What do I do?" She went on to say, "The Bible doesn't interest me, and I'm not sure I believe in prayer."

"Tomorrow morning, take just a few minutes and sit quietly with your eyes closed," I replied. "Just say, 'God, I'm not sure about You, but I'd like to meet You. Here I am. What do You want to say to me?'" I was just asking for her to create a space for Him to work. What happened then amazed her. If we just give God space He delights to show up.

Training

Another way of explaining the dynamic of how spiritual disciplines work in our lives is by the metaphor of training. John Ortberg discusses this issue under the phrase "training versus trying."[4] The spiritual disciplines work because they train us wisely for the race of life. Athletes win races not because they try hard, but because they train well. They may have tremendous willpower, but if they lack training they may still finish last in the competition. Or musicians may have great willpower, but if they have not practiced, they will not perform well. For athletes and musicians, good training and practice actually result in spontaneity and freedom. If one's training has assured a good performance, it happens naturally and spontaneously, not by force of the will. In a similar manner, if one has trained well for life with God, the structure of the training has opened the life to God and He has worked. The results come freely and seemingly effortlessly.

To help put the whole issue in perspective, I suggest that the spiritual disciplines or devotional life are:

not *a way to earn merit before God.* Nothing we do can gain acceptance with Him. That comes just because He loves us and sent Jesus to save us. The spiritual disciplines are rather a response to that love or a desire to commune with that love.

not *legalistic rules.* We should never turn the spiritual disciplines into rules that we *must* follow. Rather, they are paths to communion with God. Turning them into regulations in fact makes them deadly and destroys the essence of their meaning.

not *in their outward practice a judge or indication of true spiritual life.* Knowing the devotional practice of an individual does not necessarily tell us whether the person is progressing toward God or not. Someone can do the disciplines legalistically or blindly out of a sense of obligation. Unloving people can read the Bible and, if their hearts are hard, remain unaffected. As humans with limited knowledge, we must avoid judging others.

not *effective through building our willpower.* Spiritual disciplines—followed with a seeking heart—train us so that God's transforming power can work in our lives. If we are in training with God, we become changed so that we naturally begin to have right actions toward people and events. Willpower and will worship can never change us for the long haul.

On the other hand, true practice of the spiritual disciplines:

comes from a Spirit-given seeking after God or is the result of His grace and love already working in us. In other words, the spiritual disciplines are not the way we make our way to God, but our response to His prior seeking for us and/or a hunger that He has placed within us. Recognition of this truth keeps us from legalism and obsessive rule-keeping.

opens space for God to work in us and transforms us. In our experience in which life and evil have conspired to make us too busy for what really matters, the spiritual disciplines create space, a window in time, through which God's grace can touch us, mold us, and make us anew.

trains us in righteousness. The spiritual life is a growth process and a pilgrimage or journey. Righteousness does not happen overnight. Our divine coach trainer uses the spiritual disciplines to mature us into His image.

results in holy spontaneity. Some have argued that the spiritual disciplines must begin in the spontaneity of the Spirit. Of course, some spontaneity about the specific methods of spiritual formation is needed. For certain people the practice of the disciplines is a spontaneous response to God's grace. On the other hand, one cannot "spontaneously" refuse God's training and still expect to grow. True spontaneity and freedom for an athlete or musician comes when they have trained so well that their performance then happens as second nature. Such is the result of true spiritual training.

In the spiritual disciplines one must always find the balance between structure and freedom, discipline and spontaneity, law and spirit. A certain "structure" or "order" or "rule for life" must be accepted within the grace orientation explained above, but that structure must allow plenty of room for a freedom in specifics. Such freedom takes into consideration the individual's situation, aptitude, knowledge, and temperament. We must not assume a particular spiritual practice is the model or norm for everyone. (We will discuss this general principle in more depth in chapter 13.)

God's Call to Us

With this background in mind, we can make a strong case to follow a basic structure in the practice of the spiritual disciplines. We should always remember two main facts:

God specifically calls us to training in holiness and to the disciplines. First Timothy 4:7 says: "Train yourself to be godly." The King James Version renders it: "Exercise thyself rather unto godliness." Verse 8 goes on to add that top "physical training is of some value, but godliness has value for all things, holding promise for both the present life and the life to come."

Some may see the passage as referring to the *activity* of holy living. They suggest that God (through Paul) is summoning Timothy to the practice of holy action. That may be part of it, but I think the summons is deeper than that. Holiness is a *quality* of life that can develop only through communion with the One who alone is holy. True training for holiness is not just doing holy acts, but is having our inner life transformed by regular communication with the source of all holiness in an active spiritual life.

Not only does God call us in general to training and discipline in our lives—He summons us to specific devotional actions such as corporate worship (Heb. 10:25), singing (Eph. 5:19), and giving thanks to God (verse 20).

The heart of devotional life is prayer, and the New Testament again and again urges God's people to pray. Colossians 4:2 tells us not merely to pray but to *"devote"* ourselves to prayer, being watchful and thankful. Paul admonishes *"in everything"* by prayer and petition to present our requests to God (Phil. 4:6). Elsewhere he summons us to "pray continually" for this is God's will for us (1 Thess. 5:17, 18). A reading of the New Testament clearly shows God expects His people to be serious about prayer.

Jesus and God's serious followers through the ages have practiced the spiritual disciplines. Christ began his ministry by allowing the Spirit to lead Him into the wilderness. Much has been made of His temptation there, but His overcoming came through His communion with God. The devil arrived after Jesus' 40 days of fasting (Matt. 4:2, 3) and prayer. The test followed intense communion with God. Both the communion and testing formed the foundation of Jesus' ministry.

Thus Jesus not only began His special work in prayer, but continued through His whole ministry to pray (see Mark 1:35; Matt. 14:22, 23; Luke 11:1-4). He concluded the main phase of His earthly ministry in intense prayer in Gethsemane just before His crucifixion (Matt. 26:36-46; Mark 14:32-42; Luke 22:40-46).

The early church followed His example by devoting themselves to prayer (Acts 2:42).

And it has been the case of His people down through the ages. Edward M. Bounds chronicles many of them from the Protestant tradition in his book *Power Through Prayer.* They include the great saints of God through the years from Martin Luther to John Wesley on to Billy Graham today. God's ideal is for us to reflect this tradition.

Conclusion

God uses three main catalysts to change us.[5] The first is that of people. Friends and even enemies can be tools in His hands to shape us. The second catalyst is circumstances. The experiences of life, both good and bad, are instruments of the divine to mold and shape us. The first two catalysts are mainly out of our control. We cannot manage or dictate to all the people that we encounter in life. Certainly the circumstances in life are also, in large part, beyond our control. Because we do have a choice whether to practice them or not, we can control the third catalyst: the spiritual disciplines. They also differ from the other two in that spiritual disciplines work from the inside out, not from the outside in. Should we not take seriously this God-given path to transformation?

Rightly understood, the disciplines are not a legalistic burden to bear, but an avenue of grace to train us into the way of godliness and freedom. Following that path of life brings joy, not sorrow; peace, not stress; and hope, not despair. In short, it is the way to truly living. Please decide to use this God-given path.

---

[1] Richard Foster, *Celebration of Discipline*, p. 7.

[2] *Ibid.*

[3] Donald Postema, *Space for God* (Grand Rapids: Bible Way, 1983).

[4] John Ortberg, *The Life You've Always Wanted* (Grand Rapids: Zondervan, 1997), pp. 45-62.

[5] Donald S. Whitney, *Spiritual Disciplines for the Christian Life* (Colorado Springs, Colo.: NavPress, 1991), pp. 17, 18.

Chapter 13

What Are the Stages of Growth?

"In the past several years, I have come to realize my spiritual struggle is directly related to my desire to control God."

"It is more important for me that I walk daily with God than it is to reach a destination."

—Fellow Spiritual Pilgrims

The Growth Process

In all biological development we trace stages of progression. A seed sprouts and grows, and the resulting plant eventually becomes fully developed. Babies are conceived, born, and mature to adulthood. It makes sense to ask whether the spiritual life also has stages of growth. I believe they do exist, and we will look at them in this chapter.

The Bible uses the metaphor of *biological* growth to describe the Christian life. Growth implies a gradual change, not an instantaneous and complete transformation. "This is what the kingdom of God is like. A man scatters seed on the ground. Night and day, whether he sleeps or gets up, the seed sprouts and grows, though he does not know how. All by itself the soil produces again—first the stalk, then the head, then the full kernel in the head. As soon as the grain is ripe, he puts the sickle to it, because the harvest has come" (Mark 4:26-29).

Plant growth happens because of the life in the seed and the roles of the soil, sun, and rain. The power of God's message is the seed, and the mysterious work of God in the life through the means of grace, in large part by spiritual disciplines, brings growth and maturity. The sower does not make it happen or even understand the details of what is taking place, but nurtures the process and enjoys its benefits.

The fact that it is a gradual growth process should make us patient in the Christian walk. We cannot expect instant maturity from ourselves or others when responding to God's call. The decision to seek God starts, not ends growth. It is the introduction, not the conclusion. Not only our growth is envisioned, but that of others as well. The blessings that God gives His people when they commune with Him He then expects them to use specifically to help others grow and mature (see Eph. 4:7-13; note especially verse 13). As we work to aid others to mature, Ephesians makes clear, it assists us to grow even more.

The growth aspect of the spiritual life is so crucial that contemporary writer M. Robert Mulholland, Jr., makes it the first of the four elements in his definition of spiritual formation.[1] It helps us realize that we are on a dynamic journey. A decision made to serve Jesus five years ago is not enough for today. That decision must be a growing, maturing seed or it will die. We must say no to our desire for instant spiritual gratification and be prepared for a lifelong journey with God.

Yes, we may experience growth spurts and times of more rapid progress. We rejoice in those times, but we should not let them seduce us to the point that we think they have brought us to maturity. They are steps in God's lifelong plan for us. As we grow spiritually the road will be bumpy. When we progress, we come to understand that the tough places are normal parts of growth and that God can use them.

It is only natural, then, that humans have tried to explain or outline some of the stages of the spiritual journey or growth process. Just as biologists can describe the stages of plant or animal growth, students of the spiritual life have made the same attempt. In what follows I mention four different major attempts to portray the stages of the journey that have been helpful to spiritual pilgrims. We can view such explanations with their accompanying stages as either the *overall path* of our journey toward God or as the path toward wholeness in any *specific given area* of our lives.

I begin by explaining in more detail the path that I find most beneficial. Following that I briefly mention three other ways of explaining the journey that some consider helpful.

Peck's Stages

I regard the work of psychiatrist M. Scott Peck as very helpful for the average person seeking to understand the spiritual journey. In lectures and at least two books he has expounded his four-stage theory.[2]

Peck's four stages are:

1. The chaotic, antisocial stage, or, as Peck called it in his lecture, the "Hells Angel" phase. *2. The formal, institutional stage* in which people desire and appreciate structure. *3. The skeptical, individualization stage,* or what we could also call the agnostic stage. *4. The communal/mystical stage.*

Stage 1 people are antisocial because they care only about themselves. They are spiritually undeveloped. Their lives are chaotic because they are unprincipled. Most of them have major social problems as adults.

Most young children and perhaps one in five adults are in this stage. Some bright adults learn to do the expedient thing and function well in society, but remain unprincipled and at stage 1. Behind the scenes they make all decisions based on preserving themselves and are extremely manipulative.

Eventually most people realize that this first stage is basically chaotic and unproductive. Often the dawning of that realization is sudden, and a transformation takes place. Many times it involves a religious conversion. For some the conversion may be to another structure, such as a highly organized business or the military. Such "converted people" love the new structure, because it has given shape and meaning to a life that was previously in disarray. Many church members are at this stage. We label this stage institutional, because people have become attached to the institution or structure of the church, and formal, because they are wedded to the forms or structures of religion. That is why church members tend to get upset over changes in such things as liturgy or order of service. New Bible translations and innovative forms of music will greatly upset stage 2 people. To them it seems as if they are slipping back into the chaos they escaped from. Stage 2 people serve a God who is basically external to them. The idea of God living in them may be acceptable in theory, but in practice is hard to actualize.

Children growing up in relatively stable and loving homes often do not go through stage 1 in a rebellious way, but naturally become socialized into the faith of their parents. Having internalized the basic principles of their parents, they are comfortable at stage 2.

Some stay at stage 2 their whole lives, but many others move on to stage 3 (skeptical), a transition that often happens in adolescence. Young people begin to question the simple answers they have received as children from parents or teachers. It may happen later in life for others, who suddenly find themselves confronted with new intellectual challenges or flagrant inconsistencies in a trusted institution or structure. Whatever the case, those who once seemed settled in faith now have doubts. It is highly disturbing to parents and friends and often disconcerting to the doubters themselves.

With love, understanding, nurture, and the grace of God, many are able to move on to the fourth stage. Peck's word "mystical" may sound dangerous to some, but by it he means two things. First, such fourth-stage people see an interconnection beneath the surface of things. They begin to connect what they have learned and experienced in new ways and at deeper levels than they had previously recognized. God fits with more and more of their lives. Second, mystical has at its roots the word "mystery." People at this stage can live with mystery. Not all questions can be answered in our lives, but God does have an explanation, and we can live life trusting those mysteries to Him.

Communal in nature, such people naturally reach beyond the selfish borders of individualism and by their service and caring touch the lives of those around them.

We need to remember several things about stage theory. First, people of any age can be at any stage. Although certain ages tend to congregate at particular stages, I have seen children who very early can manifest characteristics of stage 4 while some adults never emerge from stage 1. Second, people can regress, or "backslide." If those attempting to move to stage 3 get battered too hard, they may retreat to stage 1. An unloving stage 2 home can push kids back to the Hells Angel stage. Third, we all maintain vestiges of earlier stages in our lives. As Peck says, "I have a wild Scotty caged up in my basement." In times of stress or crisis, the temptation to behave at an earlier stage is always there. Fourth, stage theory points up the challenge of communicating before a group. For a number of years I taught college religion classes composed of students at all four stages. Stages 1 and 4 were not too hard to deal with. Most stage 1 people either tuned out or once in a while complained. Stage 4 individuals can perceive what's going on and cheer you on. The bigger issue is those at stages 2 and 3. Stage 2 people always had vocal representatives who were recent converts. They applauded all aspects of institutionalized religion and were orthodoxy enforcers. After all, the church had saved them from chaos, and they felt grateful and loyal to it. Another large segment of the class had been raised at stage 2 and were now asking questions and entering into the characteristics of stage 3. Those two groups often misunderstood each other. The questions of stage 3 were heretical to stage 2, and the rigorous applauding of all details of formal religion by stage 2 was hopelessly naive to stage 3. How do you affirm *both* and encourage *both* to move on with God? I guess that's why we believe in the Holy Spirit! The aim of a church or especially a Christian college should be to guide people from stages 1 and 2 to stage 4 without losing them at stage 3.

Peck suggests that we are best able to help people who are in the previous stage to us. In most cases I think that is true. The best evangelist for stage 1 people is a stage 2 person, and so on. The important thing to remember is that God's grace is everywhere present. Salvation is *not* based on stage of development, and I expect to see some from all levels in God's kingdom. God's plan for us, however, is that we continue to grow, and we are most happy and fulfilled if we do.

Three Other Ways of Describing the Journey

The oldest of the other three methods of describing the spiritual journey is the *classical* one. Several writers in the Middle Ages quite clearly articulated it, but it is based on earlier tradition.[3] In modern times the Anglican laywoman Evelyn Underhill added to the original three steps a fourth one. Some modern writers on the spiritual life utilize this theory. *The four stages in this theory are awakening, purgation (cleansing), illumination, and finally union with God.*

While this explanation is helpful to some people, I find spiritual neophytes somewhat mystified—especially about the last step. The terminology is unfamiliar to many, and the path seems to be at a level far beyond what they can ever think of. As one student said: "You've got to be a monk to do this." For many the classical path is best discussed in depth after some spiritual growth has taken place.

Faith development is the term for the second of this group of descriptions of spiritual pilgrimage. Probably no one in the late twentieth century did more in trying to understand the growth of faith than James Fowler. Fowler builds on the French psychologist Jean Piaget, who studied logical and cognitive development in children. He then interacted with Lawrence Kohlberg and others, who moved Piaget's insights from the area of cognitive development to the moral and ethical realm. The theory Fowler built is impressive.[4] His work attempts to illustrate the stages of faith that people progress through as they grow spiritually. He sees six stages that, in many cases, have been subdivided into sublevels or steps.[5]

For those deeply interested in the topic, Fowler's work offers much insight. But for the average person the theory is complex and the vocabulary hard to understand. My work has been mainly with adults. The continuing emphasis in Fowler on age and life cycle, while helpful to those working with children and young people, is not particularly beneficial for understanding those over the age of 20.

A third possible way exists to define the stages of growth in the life of faith. In 1995 Janet O. Hagberg and Robert Guelich published a book called *The Critical Journey: Stages in the Life of Faith.*[6] Hagberg is an author and social activist, and Guelich is a New Testament scholar. Their six stages progress from stage one, the recognition of God, to stage six, which they call the life of love. One of the parts of their scheme is the honest facing of "the wall,"[7] or what others call the dark night of the soul. Clearly for them struggle and doubt can demonstrate progress in the spiritual walk. For those interested in this subject their book is must reading.

How to Take the Next Step

One question remains to be answered. What motivates a person to advance from one stage to another? A Christian might say, "How are we 'converted' from one step to the next?" The answer is not an easy one, but let me in conclusion make a few suggestions.

Obviously some changes can take place gradually in small increments. God can work in our lives and bring slow, almost imperceptible change. On the other hand, the Bible speaks often of crises. Stories of dramatic conversion and major change abound from the call of Abraham to the Damascus road experience of Paul. Certainly "God-induced calls and messages" often are major turning points, but I would go further. Times of crisis and conflict—even if they do not seem at first to be divinely initiated—offer special opportunities for growth.[8] A conflict or crisis faced with persistence and a willingness to learn is a God-graced moment for growth. The loss of a job, fiancé, spouse, or parent; the disappointment when a cherished dream vanishes; the onset of cancer or a physical malady; financial loss; or the betrayal of a friend—they are all opportunities for us to let God change us. Are we willing to grow from them? Being diagnosed with lymphoma just recently was a crisis physically, emotionally, and spiritually for me. Yet my growth has been painful but real. I believe all crises share this element of God-given potential.

Are we willing to do the analysis of our own lives that can be the gateway to growth and transformation? We must ask ourselves, Where are we now and where does God want us to grow next?

Needless to say, who we are and where we are in the growth process strongly affects our spiritual life. A commitment to seek the filling of our hunger for God will contribute greatly to our growth.

---

[1] M. Robert Mulholland, Jr., *Invitation to a Journey* (Downers Grove, Ill.: InterVarsity Press, 1993), pp. 12, 15, 19-24.

[2] See M. Scott Peck, *The Different Drum* (New York: Simon and Schuster, 1987), pp. 186-208, and *Further Along the Road Less Traveled* (New York: Simon and Schuster, 1988), pp. 119-134.

[3] Benedict J. Groeschel, *Spiritual Passages: The Psychology of Spiritual Development* (New York: Crossroad, 1986), p. 194. Pages 194-196 give a short historical survey of this teaching.

[4] We could cite a number of his books, but the place to start is probably James W. Fowler, *Stages of Faith: The Psychology of Human Development and the Quest for Meaning* (San Francisco: Harper and Row, 1981). A good summary is found in Fowler's "Life/Faith Patterns: Structures of Trust and Loyalty," in Jerome Berryman, ed., *Life Maps: Conversations on the Journey of Faith* (Waco, Tex.: Word, 1978), pp. 14-101.

[5] The six stages are the intuitive-projective, mystic-literal, synthetic conventional, individuative-reflexive, paradoxical-consolidative, and finally universalizing.

[6] Salem, Wis.: Sheffield Pub. Co. In 2005 a revised edition came out.

[7] *Ibid.*, pp.113-130.

[8] For a theoretical basis for this and the steps involved, see James E. Loder, "Transformation in Christian Education," in Jeff Astley, Leslie J. Francis, and Colin Crowder, eds., *Theological Perspectives on Christian Formation* (Grand Rapids: Eerdmans, 1996), pp. 270-284.

Chapter 14

What Should I Do Now?

"I have seen in myself that I don't possess the faith to bridge every chasm of faith."

"When my relationship with God was at its best was when it was simple."

—Fellow Spiritual Pilgrims

The material you have just studied has sought to do more than supply facts and give theoretical knowledge. The ultimate hope is to change lives and make a difference in how we relate to God. Because of that, it seems appropriate to conclude the discussion by talking about how we can continue to grow and put into our lives the values and practices shared here. What can we do to keep on maturing in Christ? How can we have a closer relationship next year than we have had the past one? I offer seven specific guidelines:

Be convicted of the theological and experiential centrality of the spiritual life. For many Western Christians the unspoken assumption is that the core of their religion is correct doctrine or belief. The important thing a Christian can do is to think right about God. Many Christians also believe that true Christianity is proper ethics or behavior. That is, certain kinds of actions or nonaction are the key to Christianity. While I would never deny that theology and ethics are important, they cannot stand above the role of the heart and the centrality of love. Jesus saw plenty of true believers and right-doers in his day, but He was looking for something else. He wanted heart-to-heart communion that sensed the awesome truth that God is with us and wants to communicate with us and relate to us. That is why He commended Mary, who sat at His feet and listened, as doing the one thing needful, and gently revealed to her busy sister Martha that her anxious "doing" was not the best path to follow.

Somehow this truth—that the living out of a devotional life that truly communes with God is the foundation for right belief—must become established in our hearts and minds. It is the root that alone can bear the true fruit. If we can be convinced of this, then the discipline of setting priorities, finding time, and persevering becomes a sacred call.

Notice the fruits of true spirituality. Everything we do has results of some kind. Our practice of the spiritual life is no exception. Taking the time to look at some of the specific positive fruits that are in progress in our life can help us keep going, just as noticing how exercise has bettered our body provides incentive to continue on a workout program.

In my own experience and that of my students, truly grasping the insight that we can actually commune with God and that He speaks to us is pivotal. If we catch that vision, even our first perhaps bumbling efforts give us an often surprising sense of divine presence and nearness. Our view of faith need not abandon the rational, but moves on to actually feel God's presence. That sense is something money can't buy. I am not saying every day is a glorious "aha" experience, but such experiences will come more often and give meaning to life as nothing else can.

Joy and celebration are also fruits of a genuine walk with God. The gospel is, after all, "good news," and good news, by its very nature, brings joy. If, in fact, God loves us so much that He wants to communicate with us; if, in fact, He has conquered death and sin; and if, in fact, in His grace we are accepted as His beloved in spite of ourselves, joy and celebration will then spring up naturally. They cannot be suppressed.

Jesus loved a party. His first miracle was at a wedding feast and served to extend the festivity (John 2:1-11). When questioned why He didn't fast as the Pharisees, He compared His whole time of ministry here on earth to that of a wedding celebration (Mark 2:18-20). Once we meet this Jesus through the spiritual disciplines we cannot help receiving joy.

Some people, recognizing that the Bible teaches joy as part of the Christian life, try to promote it artificially or prematurely. But it cannot be manufactured. Joy comes as a result of meeting and following Jesus as He really is, and that occurs through the spiritual disciplines.

The psalms are wonderful examples of true balance. They have complaints, sadness, and mourning, but when the psalmist encounters God in the end, there is not simply quiet joy, but seemingly unbridled celebration. It involves singing, dancing, shouting, and the playing of all manner of musical instruments.

Laughter can be holy. In fact, I believe that only the one who has experienced God's grace can freely laugh. Too many of us laugh at ourselves and others only halfheartedly. Our weakness and theirs are too painful and too real. On the other hand, if we have honestly faced our needs and still experienced the grace and acceptance of God, we can laugh with abandon in the presence of a Jesus who also laughed.

Growth is also a fruit of the disciplines. Just as weeding and fertilizing produces better plants over time, so the spiritual disciplines grow better Christians. Time and again, students in their evaluations of the class in spiritual formation look back on its three to four months and rejoice over the growth that has taken place in all kinds of ways in their lives. You may just be less touchy when criticized or more patient with problems that arise. Or you may move less frenetically and have more hope. Growth comes in many forms.

The spiritual disciplines also promote service. Having met God, we are able to see His love for His other children more clearly and be led to act on it. I heard Ron Sider say in his discussion of social activism during the 1960s that those who agitated for civil rights from the basis of a political belief or social fad were by the 1980s mostly stockbrokers—an occupation they had earlier hated. The only ones who still worked for justice were committed Christians who served out of their religious experience. Meeting God creates a sustained commitment to service and love for others.

Strange as it may seem, service also can work in the other direction. Ministering to others can drive us back to the spiritual disciplines. As we see needs that we feel inadequate to fill, as we see our limited capacity for love, patience, and giving, it compels us back to God. He alone can fit us for ministry and intervene in the lives of others to bring needed change.

Service, then, is both a fruit and a root of the spiritual disciplines and a key part of the Christian life.

Be honest with God. The longer I live, the more I see in myself and in others the capacity for self-deception.* In most cases we don't intend to be that way. We must deliberately set up barriers against slipping into it.

One way to do so is to follow some of the suggestions given in the preceding pages. A yearly retreat gives an individual time to reflect on spiritual progress. Accountability through regular participation in small groups as well as meeting with a mentor or spiritual counselor to whom we give permission to probe our life will all help us to be honest.

Evaluation on a regular basis will protect us from ourselves. We should set goals for ourselves and then plan to examine ourselves periodically. One way to do that faithfully is to keep records. As I mentioned previously, during any teaching of spiritual formation, I require students to log actual time spent in spiritual disciplines. Some will always argue that such record keeping detracts from true devotion and thus hinders growth. But many in the end thank me because such recording day by day reveals the truth about how much time they are really spending with God. Willingness to face honestly how we are doing helps us make needed changes and keeps us teachable.

Recognize the key role of the Holy Spirit. According to the New Testament, the one thing the first followers of Jesus were to wait and pray for was the Holy Spirit's presence (Acts 1:8). The reception of the Spirit created the dynamic early church and led the apostles who had experienced His presence to promise it to others (Acts 2:38). John the Baptist had baptized with water, but Jesus baptized with the Holy Spirit (Mark 1:8). That Holy Spirit is the divine dynamic behind everything in the spiritual life. The hunger for God that drives us to seek Him, the power of Christian community, the urge to pray, and the joy of worship all stem from the Spirit.

The ongoing presence of the Spirit is what will make us grow in all the spiritual disciplines. We would do well continually to seek ongoing fullness of the Spirit as the power source for spiritual growth.

I simply remind you of several theological/spiritual truths. The Holy Spirit is a person with power, not simply an impersonal force. He is Jesus' continuing presence with us. Through the Spirit, Jesus continues to teach and bless us. As such, the dynamic of communion with God is a personal relationship of love, not simply a mechanical reception of divine force. When the Spirit is present, we sense Jesus' presence. And the Spirit's presence leads us to pray. As we like to be where we are cherished and desired, so it is with the Spirit. I find it crucial to begin any devotional time that seeks to encounter God with a heartfelt appeal for the Spirit to be present. Do you want to grow spiritually? Seek the Spirit. If you don't understand what that involves, by all means find out. Your Christian growth depends on it.

Keep reading, studying, and listening to learn more about the spiritual life. I have included a bibliography for the various topics covered in this book. While I could have cited more titles, I have deliberately tried to select what I believe are some of the best. I hope you'll read some of them.

When I finished the seminary, I found that I had a substantial library in three areas—biblical studies, practical theology (mainly preaching), and systematic theology. In addition I had a smattering of books on church history and biblical languages. That summarized my theological education. It had emphasized biblical studies, theology, and preaching. Nothing was there on the topics of the spiritual life, such as prayer and meditation. And spiritual biography was absent. Fortunately, I think education for ministry may be changing into a more balanced approach.

I particularly believe that biography can be helpful. Reading the stories of spiritual pilgrims from old classics such as *The Practice of the Presence of God,* by Brother Lawrence, to more recent works, such as Thomas Kelly's *Testament of Devotion* and Garth Maclean's *On the Tail of a Comet* (about the life of Frank Buchman) have inspired and transformed me. I have specifically included these and other biographies in my bibliography. The story of lived spirituality has a power to motivate that books on mere theory lack.

Seek mentorship and spiritual guidance. The expression "spiritual guide" may wave red flags to some Protestants, but it need not do so. A spiritual guide is not an authority who tells us exactly what we should do, but, as a fellow pilgrim, listens to us and tries to help us on our way. If the term truly bothers you, use the word "mentor." It implies someone of experience who can help us grow in the knowledge and practice of the disciplines. Strange as it may seem, in Christian circles it may be more acceptable to use a psychological counselor than a spiritual counselor. Both can be helpful.

Seeking a mentor or spiritual guide is not an indication of spiritual weakness but a sign of an openness and willingness to grow. Perhaps it might be even better to use the phrase "soul friend." Then we can see clearly that having someone to be friends with for the purpose of more intimately encountering God is both valid and desirable.

One of the great tragedies is that people who are qualified and willing to do this may be hard to find. Training programs in Protestant Christianity to prepare such people are rare. Some pastors or counselors may fit the role, while others may not. Careful thought and honest prayer need to go into the decision to approach someone to fill such a role in your life, but finding the right person can be extremely helpful and rewarding.

Submission signified by specific commitment is crucial. Submission is not a popular word today. Talk about it seems to militate against such terms in our culture as self-actualization and freedom. One cannot, however, avoid the truth that Scripture urges submission.

Paul calls upon Christians to "be subject to one another out of reverence for Christ" (Eph. 5:21). This follows on our submission to God (James 4:7), which Jesus obviously models when He says to God, "Not as I will, but as thou wilt" (Matt. 26:39, KJV). Jesus came to minister to and give His life for others (Mark 10:49; Phil. 2:6-11). Early Christians did not see exceptions to the rule: "All of you be subject one to another" (1 Peter 5:5, KJV).

Christians, therefore, base their submission on the model and command of Jesus. The gospel message has freed us from any subordinate status. The Son (Jesus) has made us free. Slave and master, president and common laborer, all share the same status before God and are brothers and sisters in Christ. Because we know that we are free, we then can voluntarily submit both to God and to others. Submission, of course, can become warped or misguided. It has limits that may sometimes be a challenge to define. In general, however, Christians should submit to the clear will of God and to human authority as long as it is not destructive or counter to God's will.

Submission is related to obedience. When we decide to obey, we are submitting ourselves to the commands given us, and, for a Christian, that should be to the command of love.

How does all of this relate to the subject of this book and the disciplines of the spiritual life? God's call to us is to love, to worship, and to obey Him. The most direct way we do this is by connecting with Him, and that happens best through the avenue of the spiritual disciplines that He has given to us. To neglect those pathways is to refuse to submit to and obey God's basic will for us. We submit by specifically committing to what we will regularly do to enhance our communion with Him. To wait until we "feel like it" or are "inspired" to do it or are "impressed" to is to trust ourselves to the changing moods we have. Submission to time and place frees us from looking at how we "feel" and gives structure and concreteness to our commitment to God. It's much like taking a pill necessary for our health. The doctor has said that we need it daily, but we decide we'll take it when we are impressed to or when we feel like it. That sets up a challenging situation. We try to decide if we are impressed or not impressed, and every pill-taking requires a new decision.

The best spiritual plan is to decide to commune with God and submit to His will. Specifically set time parameters, and be as regular as you are at eating. This decision to submit will provide a structure that enables God to work in your life in ways that you may not have dreamed possible.

I believe a life of communing with God is an exciting and transforming experience. The rewards are both in this world and out of this world. For your own sake and for God's kingdom, please seriously pursue the journey, and you will find your spiritual hunger satisfied.

---

* M. Scott Peck, *People of the Lie*, gives an in-depth look at this issue.

For Further Reading—Selected Bibliography

Christian Spiritual Formation

1. General

Benner, David G. *Surrender to Love.* Downers Grove, Ill.: InterVarsity Press, 2003.

Boa, Kenneth. *Conformed to His Image.* Grand Rapids: Zondervan, 2001.

Calhoun, Adele Ahlberg. *Spiritual Disciplines Handbook.* Downers Grove, Ill.: InterVarsity, 2005.

Chan, Simon. *Spiritual Theology: A Systematic Study of the Christian Life.* Downers Grove, Ill.: InterVarsity, 1998.

Edwards, Tilden. *Living in the Presence: Disciplines for the Spiritual Heart.* New York: Harper and Row, 1988.

Foster, Richard. *Celebration of Discipline.* New York: Harper and Row, 1988.

Issler, Klaus. *Wasting Time With God.* Downers Grove, Ill.: InterVarsity, 2001.

Kelsey, Morton. *Encounter With God.* Minneapolis: Bethany Fellowship, 1972.

Leech, Kenneth. *Experiencing God: Theology as Spirituality.* New York: Harper and Row, 1985.

Maas, Robin, and Gabriel O'Donnell. *Spiritual Traditions for the Contemporary Church.* Nashville: Abingdon, 1990.

McNeal, Reggie. *A Work of Heart.* San Francisco: Jossey-Bass, 2000.

Mulholland, M. Robert, Jr. *Invitation to a Journey.* Downers Grove, Ill.: InterVarsity Press, 1993.

Nouwen, Henri J. M. *Making All Things New: An Invitation to the Spiritual Life.* New York: HarperCollins, 1981.

Peterson, Eugene H. *A Long Obedience in the Same Direction: Discipleship in an Instant Society*. Downers Grove, Ill.: InterVarsity, 1980.

White, Ellen G. *Steps to Christ*. Mountain View, Calif.: Pacific Press, 1956.

Whitney, Donald S. *Spiritual Disciplines for the Christian Life*. Colorado Springs, Colo.: NavPress, 1991.

Willard, Dallas. *The Spirit of the Disciplines: Understanding How God Changes Lives*. New York: Harper and Row, 1988.

2. Autobiography-Devotional

Bacovcin, Helen, trans. *The Way of a Pilgrim: And the Pilgrim Continues His Way*. New York: Image Books, 1978.

Hinson, E. Glenn, ed. *The Doubleday Devotional Classics* (journals of George Fox, David Brainerd, and John Woolman). New York: Doubleday, 1978. Vol. 2.

Kelly, Thomas R. *A Testament of Devotion*. New York: HarperCollins, 1992.

Lawrence, Brother. *The Practice of the Presence of God*. Old Tappan, N.J.: Fleming H. Revell, 1958.

Thomas à Kempis. *Of the Imitation of Christ*. New York: New American Library, 1957.

Watson, David. *You Are My God: A Pioneer of Renewal Recounts His Pilgrimage in Faith*. Wheaton, Ill.: Harold Shaw, 1984.

3. Temperament and Spirituality

Goldsmith, Malcolm. *Knowing Me, Knowing God: Exploring Your Spirituality With Myers-Briggs*. Nashville: Abingdon, 1997.

Keating, Charles J. *Who We Are Is How We Pray: Matching Personality and Spirituality*. Mystic, Conn.: Twenty-third Publications, 1987.

Keirsey, David, and Marilyn Bates. *Please Understand Me*. Del Mar, Calif.: Prometheus Nemesis, 1984.

Oswald, Roy M., and Otto Kroeger. *Personality Type and Religious Leadership*. New York: Alban Institute, 1988.

Richardson, Peter Tufts. *Four Spiritualities: Expressions of Self, Expressions of Spirit.* Palo Alto, Calif.: Davies-Black, 1996.

Rohr, Richard, Andreas Ebert, et al. *Experiencing the Enneagram.* New York: Crossroad, 1992.

4. Worship

Allen, Ronald B., and Gordon Borror. *Worship: Rediscovering the Missing Jewel.* Portland, Oreg.: Multnomah, 1982.

Carothers, Merlin. *Prison to Praise.* Escondido, Calif.: Merlin R. Carothers, 1970.

Hayford, Jack W. *Worship His Majesty.* Waco, Tex.: Word, 1987.

Ortlund, Anne. *Up With Worship.* Ventura, Calif.: Regal, 1975.

Webber, Robert E. *Worship Is a Verb.* Waco, Tex.: Word, 1985.

5. Confession and Repentance

Augsburger, David W. *Helping People Forgive.* Louisville, Ky.: Westminster John Knox, 1996.

McCullough, Michael E., Steven J. Sandage, Everett L. Worthington, Jr. *To Forgive Is Human: How to Put Your Past in the Past.* Downers Grove, Ill.: InterVarsity, 1997.

Miller, J. Keith. *A Hunger for Healing: The Twelve Steps as a Classic Model for Christian Spiritual Growth.* New York: HarperCollins, 1991.

Seamands, David A. *Healing of Memories.* Colorado Springs, Colo.: ChariotVictor, 1985.

6. Prayer

Baillie, John. *A Diary of Private Prayer.* New York: Charles Scribner's Sons, 1949.

Bounds, E. M. *Power Through Prayer.* London: Marshall Brothers, Ltd., n.d.

Duewel, Wesley L. *Mighty Prevailing Prayer.* Grand Rapids: Zondervan, 1990.

Engelkemier, Joe. *Whatever It Takes Praying: How Our Yes to What God Asks Brings His Yes to What We Ask.* Fallbrook, Calif.: Hart Research Center, 1993.

Foster, Richard J. *Prayer: Finding the Heart's True Home.* New York: HarperCollins, 1992.

Hallesby, O. *Prayer.* Minneapolis: Augsburg Fortress, 1994.

Shewmake, Carrol Johnson. *Practical Pointers to Personal Prayer.* Washington, D.C.: Review and Herald, 1989.

Linn, Dennis, Matthew Linn, and Sheila Fabricant. *Prayer Course for Healing Life's Hurts.* New York: Paulist, 1983.

7. Meditation

Capps, Walter Holden, and Wendy M. Wright. *Silent Fire: An Invitation to Western Mysticism.* New York: Harper and Row, 1978.

DeMello, Anthony. *Sadhana: A Way to God—Christian Exercises in Eastern Form.* New York: Image, 1978.

Huggett, Joyce. *The Joy of Listening to God.* Downers Grove, Ill.: InterVarsity, 1987.

Kaisch, Ken. *Finding God: A Handbook of Christian Meditation.* New York: Paulist, 1995.

Kaplan, Aryeh. *Jewish Meditation: A Practical Guide.* New York: Schocken Books, 1985.

Keating, Thomas. *Finding Grace at the Center.* Petersham, Mass.: St. Bede's, 1978.

McCormick, Thomas, and Sharon Fish. *Meditation.* Downers Grove, Ill.: InterVarsity, 1983.

Postema, Don. *Space for God.* Grand Rapids: Bible Way, 1983.

Toon, Peter. *From Mind to Heart: Christian Meditation Today.* Grand Rapids: Baker Book House, 1987.

8. Bible Study

Dodson, Peter. *Contemplating the Word: A Practical Handbook.* Wilton, Conn.: Morehouse-Barlow, 1987.

L'Heureux, Conrad E. *Life Journey and the Old Testament: An*

Experiential Approach to the Bible and Personal Transformation. New York: Paulist, 1986.

Mulholland, M. Robert, Jr. *Shaped by the Word: The Power of Scripture in Spiritual Formation.* Nashville: The Upper Room, 1985.

Vest, Norvene. *Bible Reading for Spiritual Growth.* New York: HarperCollins, 1993.

Weber, Hans-Ruedi. *Experiments in Bible Study.* Philadelphia: Westminster, 1981.

Wink, Walter. *Transforming Bible Study.* Nashville: Abingdon, 1980.

9. Journaling

Canham, Elizabeth. *Journaling With Jeremiah.* New York: Paulist, 1992.

Cargas, Harry J., and Roger J. Radley. *Keeping a Spiritual Journal.* Garden City, N.Y.: Nazareth, 1981.

DelBene, Ron, and Herb Montgomery. *Alone With God.* New York: Harper and Row, 1984.

Kelsey, Morton T. *Adventure Inward: Christian Growth Through Personal Journal Writing.* Minneapolis: Augsburg, 1980.

Klug, Ronald. *How to Keep a Spiritual Journal.* Minneapolis: Augsburg, 1993.

10. Lifestyle/Simplicity

Campolo, Anthony. *Ideas for Social Action: A Handbook on Mission and Service for Christian Young People.* El Cajon, Calif.: Youth Specialties, 1983.

Foster, Richard. *Freedom of Simplicity.* San Francisco: Harper and Row, 1989.

Peck, M. Scott. *The Road Less Traveled: A New Psychology of Love, Traditional Values and Spiritual Growth.* New York: Simon and Schuster, 1978.

Sider, Ron. *Rich Christians in an Age of Hunger.* Downers Grove, Ill.: InterVarsity, 1984.

Sine, Tom. *The Mustard Seed Conspiracy*. Dallas: Word, 1981.

———. *Wild Hope*. Dallas: Word, 1991.

11. Spiritual Guidance and Mentoring

Benner, David G. *Psychotherapy and the Spiritual Quest*. Grand Rapids: Baker Book, 1988.

Byrne, Lavinia, ed. *Traditions of Spiritual Guidance*. Collegeville, Minn.: Liturgical Press, 1991.

Groeschel, Benedict J. *Spiritual Passages: The Psychology of Spiritual Development*. New York: Crossroad, 1986.

Kelsey, Morton T. *Companions on the Inner Way: The Art of Spiritual Guidance*. New York: Crossroad, 1983.

Leech, Kenneth. *Soul Friend*. New York: Harper and Row, 1980.

Neufelder, Jerome M., and Mary C. Coelho, eds. *Writings on Spiritual Direction: by Great Christian Masters*. Minneapolis: Seabury Press, 1982.